Praise for Jan Frazier's *Freedom of Being*

"In *The Freedom of Being*, Jan Frazier guides us to experience the exquisite stillness outside of the illusion of time, and re-introduces us to the experience of eternity. Through reading and practicing the principles in this book we learn not only the power of being present, but also how to bring peace to each situation we encounter." —Dr. Lee Jampolsky, author of *How to Say Yes When Your Body Says No*

"Spiritual teacher, Jan Frazier, has blessed us with another life-changing, smashing book, *The Freedom of Being*. It should be the book we all get at birth—a roadmap to show us how to create a soul-satisfying life. You'll learn simple, yet effective, ways to reawaken to the splendor of YOU and carve out a life that's rich with meaning and purpose. Once I started reading this gem-of-a-book, I couldn't put it down. Every page captivated me and resonated in my heart. It also helped me feel more empowered and uplifted. A compelling book, it's the perfect present to gift my friends and family. Kudos to Jan Frazier!" — Susan Smith Jones, PhD, author of *Walking on Air* and *The Joy Factor*

"I heartily recommend Jan Frazier's *The Freedom of Being, at ease with what is*. The writing is clean, clear and bright, giving us an articulate and detailed map of the territory of awakening. Her map draws a multitude of distinctions between a life driven by ego and an awakened life, offering a look into her world as a bright guidepost for their own journey. She describes in intricate detail the interplay between the thought processes and whatever outer circumstances you find yourself in, explaining how changing those circumstances is not how to awaken. We don't need to fix our circumstances in order to be happy! Jan's teachings tell us that we awaken within whatever our circumstances are, giving us the opportunity to step into freedom in each moment. Crisis can even be an opening for awakening according to Jan and I hope her readers can apply this to the world situation at the moment, though perhaps this is more the task of my own recent book. This certainly is where our two books meet, where crisis becomes an opportunity, and where fear falls away to reveal a new vitality and a new consciousness." —Alice Gardner, author of *Life Beyond Belief* and *Finding Our Way Forward*.

Praise for Jan Frazier's *When Fear Falls Away*

"Jan Frazier's *When Fear Falls Away* is a breathing translation into language of an advance in evolution that is available to the focused heart and the fortunate intention. She speaks of the causeless joy that permeates her. She is blessed. It is noted in the annals of the science of evolution that when reptiles evolved into birds, not only did they become freed from gravity, they also became able to dream. Reptiles do not— but birds dream. Imagine what other leaps in the evolution of consciousness might lie ahead. Might there be an evolution into mercy and awareness, into causeless joy and simple clarity?" —Stephen Levine, author of *Unattended Sorrow: Recovering from Loss and Reviving the Heart*

"Grace still comes unbidden. It's time we listened." —Larry Dossey, M.D., author of *The Extraordinary Healing Power of Ordinary Things*

"This book will change your life. Line after line holds an idea you will return to for clarity and peace from this day forward. I found myself breathing in sighs of relief coupled with peace while reading and I will love rereading it because of how it made me feel. The hope that what happened to Jan Frazier can happen to all of us is guaranteed. As she says so eloquently, 'the recognition of choice' is all that's really necessary." —Karen Casey, PhD, author of *Each Day a New Beginning*

"In *When Fear Falls Away,* Jan Frazier shows us the anatomy of epiphany and reminds us of the ever-present possibility of healing and freedom and grace. This book is a nightlight." —Rachel Naomi Remen, MD, author of *Kitchen Table Wisdom* and *My Grandfather's Blessings*

"Read this delicious, liberating, radical book. It offers the best of gifts, finding the joy and love of your own freedom." —Jack Kornfield, author of *A Path with Heart*

"If you have ever wondered if a life filled with freedom and free of fear was possible, then this is the book for you. Jan Frazier shares her personal journey with a level of intimacy normally saved for one's closest confidants. The result is a book that serves as a beacon for anyone who is ready to experience joy on every level." —Shelly Rachanow, author of *If Women Ran the World, Sh*t Would Get Done*

The Freedom
of Being

*at ease with
what is*

JAN FRAZIER

WEISER BOOKS
San Francisco, CA / Newburyport, MA

First published in 2012 by Weiser Books
Red Wheel/Weiser, LLC
With offices at:
665 Third Street, Suite 400
San Francisco, CA 94107
www.redwheelweiser.com

ISBN: 978-1-57863-517-7

Library of Congress Cataloging-in-Publication Data

Frazier, Jan.
The freedom of being / by Jan Frazier.
    p. cm.
Includes bibliographical references (p.   ) and index.
ISBN 978-1-57863-517-7 (alk. paper)
1. Life. 2. Human beings. 3. Philosophical anthropology. 4. Spirituality.
BD431.F683 2012
113'.8--dc23
                                        2012012159

Cover design by Jim Warner
Interior by Jane Hagaman
Typeset in Bembo and Gill Sans

Printed in the United States of America
C
10 9 8 7 6 5 4 3 2 1

The paper used in this publication meets the minimum requirements of the American National Standard for Information Sciences—Permanence of Paper for Printed Library Materials Z39.48-1992 (R1997).

This book is dedicated to the earth's beloved creatures (who have no need of it). Animals know what it is to simply live. Observing them, we sense what's possible for ourselves.

We shall not cease from exploration
And the end of all our exploring
Will be to arrive where we started
And know the place for the first time.

—T. S. ELIOT

Contents

Part Three: The Solitary Traveler, with No Place to Go

Invitation to the Reader

It is an expression of faith that you've picked up this book. There's an intuition of something beyond what you presently experience as reality. Maybe it's the hundredth book you've turned to, looking for a way to see. Perhaps you have despaired. Maybe things are better than before, but you want to keep going.

Chances are you long ago stopped blaming everything on bad luck. On karma, childhood, lousy genes, or the alignment of the stars. (If you're still blaming those things, it's not too late to stop.) Chances are you've assumed at least some responsibility for your inner life, or you wouldn't be reading these words.

You might have been wanting to wake up for a long time. Maybe it's a new thing for you; maybe you have only the vaguest notion of what "waking up" means. Wherever you are, you're among the few courageous enough to confront yourself, to put to yourself the fundamental question:

What is this life?

How must you live so that when it comes time to be done, you'll know you didn't miss the primary thing?

How can you live in such a way that experience, in all its rich and complicated variety, is felt more as delight than as burden—whether or not a radical awakening comes about?

You may have been asking these things, with varying answers, for a long time.

This book means to open you to possibility beyond what you've known thus far. It means to draw you closer not to certainty, but to comfort in the absence of answers.

Wherever you are, however hard you have tried, however many times you've switched directions, or given up, start fresh.

Here, now.

Be still. Let yourself rest from all the effort. From thinking you know something. Feel that you are here, that you exist: just that. Feel the restfulness there.

Imagine not being at the mercy of your mind, your history. Imagine being saturated in attention—in plain, unadorned presence. In *being* that's aware of itself.

What if that were the whole thing? What if you didn't have to work so hard?

What if you didn't have to die to get to heaven?

Introduction

Was it lucky, or does it mean nothing at all, that one of the earth's creatures happened to grow in such a way that it could know itself? That it had the capacity to lose this knowledge, then be restored to it, and call that homecoming heaven? The raccoon does not do this. It never lost itself. But then, the raccoon cannot experience *being* that's aware of itself. The raccoon isn't endowed with what we are—which carries with it the ability to while away a life by spending it all inside the head. It wouldn't dawn on a raccoon to do anything but what it's doing to stay alive.

Was it lucky that we evolved? That there should be a planet amenable to life (outlandishly improbable enough); that in this world, so lavishly creatured and planted, there should be one bumbling animal that managed to grow a brain so good it could do impressive things (imagine, speak, string thoughts together, invent concepts like *tomorrow, enemy*), endowing it all with the feel and taste of the real? We made that most devastating of discoveries: that it is possible to neglect to notice *that we exist*. To be so fixated on our minds' creations that the lapse in presence can sustain itself for the duration of an entire life. Thus do we lose contact with our essence, with our *being*-ness, thinking our way right out of the heaven we were born into: this persistently beating heart, the great green and blue world, the vast black between the stars—in which we miraculously exist.

We manage not to notice.

But we are still here. There is possibility yet, in the given time, to come alive, to remember ourselves. Our intelligence is wide-ranging enough to intuit that what the mind produces, what it has access to, may not be the ultimate truth. We are like our own prodigal children. Though we've become lost in all our highly evolved mental finery, the truth of what we are can be discovered anew. We can come home to the presence we were born to. The raccoon will never know the joy of the return. (It wouldn't think to leave.) But we who left—we can realize we've wandered off and (what could be more lucky?) *we can find our way back*. The joy of the return—to be had by no creature but us—exceeds every other possible joy.

The sky is not big enough to hold it.

●

It looks for all the world as though the condition a person starts with, and whatever's cobbled together from there forward, is what constitutes life. Wherever meaning or value is to be found, it must be there: in the ways we spend time, the choices we make, the things we accomplish, what takes place in the world around us. That seems to be the whole story. It all goes on for each of us, feeling quite real and important. Whatever the degree of satisfaction, life *as it is ordinarily defined* seems to be the stuff of human existence.

Yet all the while, there is the presence of something else, something real, that's independent of the life we regularly imbue with meaning. This *something* is everywhere, always, pervading all that is—including our very selves. We can fail to notice it. There might be fleeting awareness of it. Seldom is the knowing sustained. Yet this more substantial reality is persistently *here*, even as a whole life may be lived at a perceived distance from this most extraordinary thing attending each moment.

This primal condition is the source, the fulfillment, of every longing—of everything we try, in our ordinary lives, to bring about by familiar means. We look for it in relationship, in creativity, in achievement, in the life of the intellect, in physical challenge (mountain climbing, marathons). We seek it in the accumulation of experience, in systems of belief, in the dreamed-of future. We imagine it awaits us in the afterlife. Oh, the sad irony. We look for it outside ourselves, in the insubstantial, the transitory, where it will never be found. All the while, this unconditional delight, this unwoundable state of well-being, is the essence of our nature.

How can we possibly miss it? We have trouble turning from the usual suspects to satisfy the deep ache for wholeness, fulfillment, truth. We can't help thinking love will do it, or good health, or attainment of one thing or another. Perhaps being needed will do it, or being useful, or earning recognition. We look past what is already here, within, waiting for us to know our *selves*.

It's hard to believe there could be something more real than all a life appears to be—hard to imagine a reality both formless and more substantial than any form. A reality outside of time, subject to nothing, lacking nothing, still and unwavering and perfect, *of which a human being partakes*. How can this be? How can the experience of that *other* bring such peace, such excruciating joy, when it is made of sheer nothingness?

But so it is. This *other* has nothing to do with anything that happens in our lives. It is with us unceasingly, through all we do and fail to do. It's what we swim in, what constitutes our existence.

There are hints. It makes its presence known in stillness, in undiluted attention, in the in-betweens: between exhale and inhale, one note and the next, one thought and another; between the sound of wind and the feel of it on the skin; between two beats of the heart.

Between birth and death.

This *something* is like a liquid constantly seeking points of entry, a vapor determined to find and fill every available space. It means to permeate awareness, to be felt in the fullness of its generosity. Each moment it is here, and again *here*, awaiting discovery. So we might know that *it* is what we truly are, and know at last that all the rest (however compelling) is pale, limp, inconsequential.

●

A person might think there's nothing to be done about the life inside the cranium. It seems to carry on independent of any wish for peace that shows up around the edges. The yearning for ease and contentment is wistful. It's like the longing of a suitor pining from a distance, having no expectation of ever attaining the company of the beloved, of getting to enter the house, sit down, stay awhile. Let alone move in for keeps.

A person might suppose the mind is a closed world, a perpetual motion machine; that there can be no end to the tyranny there, the head packed with its own history, populated by its dreams and regrets, driven by its idea of what a life is supposed to look like, of how the world ought to be. It might seem it all has a will of its own, no way to occupy a life without *thinking* running the show.

The mind surely is an impressive tool, wonderfully useful. Like any tool, it has a proper function. But improper application of it can be unhealthy, even destructive. Just because the mind has enormous potential doesn't mean it ought to be allowed to run loose like a hyperactive, hormonal fourteen-year-old without a curfew.

It's not that the mind is bad. The problem is that it tends to run on automatic, a machine we can't figure out how to turn off. Most of the time, we don't even realize it's running. Its ever-looping content is like elevator music, hardly noticed, like background static that's tuned out.

Because the mind goes everywhere we go, the temptation to use it constantly is overwhelming. It runs simply because *it can*. Like a misapplied hammer, the overactive mind takes random whacks at everything in sight, omitting no opportunity to judge, balk, interpret, identify with, stew over, start a story about.

It's the rigidity and the ceaseless busy-ness of the mind that make it so hard to discern the perfect stillness of our underlying reality.

We have more to say in the matter of mental noise than we half dream. Not by going at it in a full frontal assault, but by a little sneak around to the back side, where the plug is. It can be slipped from the power supply—just by flooding the present moment with attention. Simply by *attending* what's here and now.

Don't mind whatever the here-and-now happens to be. Don't make up a story about it. Just *be* with it.

The plug slips out all by itself.

●

I might have thought I wouldn't want a life without desire, a condition cool of that terrible heat, its twin expressions: wanting and getting, having and losing. Or never having at all, *wanting* just multiplying, like a cancer cell desperate to make more of itself. I call it that now, cancer, but once upon a time, I fed on wanting. It sustained me. Needing to get something, to get somewhere, was how I felt myself exist.

I thought I needed to be separate from the lovely, ungraspable world, so I could know the effort of striving, the poignant reach *toward*. My early lessons, my touchstones, were lines of poetry, like Robert Browning's

Ah, but a man's reach should exceed his grasp,
Or what's a heaven for?

And this one by Wallace Stevens:

The imperfect is our paradise.

The finger of Adam at its slim distance from God's hand: that was my prototype. The space of not-quite was where the ache of aliveness was felt, stirring the notes of a sorrowful song, the reaching toward another human being. Beauty and wholeness seemed destined to be ephemeral, only ever approximated. Not-having was what gave rise to my own attempt at poetry. Life was about striving, the savoring of fulfillment, however brief. Each time, after loss, the renewal of hope.

I loved that life. If you'd said I could say goodbye to it, I'd have said no thanks. I'd not have wanted the emptiness that was all I could picture as an alternative. Life without longing would be an anemic thing, without warmth or color. It would, I supposed, be a kind of death.

Notwithstanding my romantic orientation to suffering (the capacity for grief being equal to the capacity for joy), there was no denying that the ideal situation would be finally to get everything I wanted, and to luxuriate in it—to live in the house of the beloved. If you'd offered me rest from fearful grasping, I'd have taken it in a heartbeat. I was making the best of an imperfect situation, consoled by the belief that the perennial dissatisfaction made me human. In any case, it was inevitable that some of the wanted things wouldn't materialize, or they'd come but wouldn't stay, so I might as well get used to it (a reasonable adaptation).

If I thought there was any remedy for the anxious middle of the night, sleep receding like a tide racing for the horizon; if I imagined an end to the worries about my children, my health, it

The Freedom of Being

was that finally things would even out, no visible bumps in the road ahead. We'd all stay okay (enough); there would be enough money; my kids would find happiness. I could finally relax. A bit. (If only it would hold.)

The trouble wasn't that I couldn't get it all to happen. The trouble was that I counted on the okayness of things to be my sustenance, the source of well-being. The trouble was that I defined myself by my circumstances and my efforts, by who I was: my children's mother, a writer of poems and supporter of other writers, a hard-working, well-meaning person. Doing well at these things was my fix. I was tethered to them like a patient with tubes snaking to clear bags dangling from portable poles. They were my sugar and salt, my way of keeping okay in this life of mine. I needed at least minimal success and stability in order to sleep well, to feel all right about myself. But sometimes these life-sustainers dried up. The very thing I'd wanted eluded me, turned bad, sickened me with my failure, with something not going as I'd hoped. Still, I was hooked up to these things that mattered, steadily fed (or starved) by how it all went. I could go nowhere, not even into sleep, that it didn't all accompany me.

Anyhow, I wouldn't have known who I was without it.

●

I did not set out to detach myself from all I drew meaning from, to slip from the seesaw of desire and loss. I was making an effort to suffer less, having some success, but I had no expectation of absolute relief.

It was as if one night I crawled into bed the person I'd always been, and in the morning woke up changed—as if, while I slept, kindly beings crept into the dark where I lay, and carried away things I'd clung to all my life. So much leaving me that I'd always thought *was* me. Yet something remained, peacefully resting, unaware a miracle was taking place. My familiar self fading away, in its place the room filled with a blessing, so that when I woke, I would know myself for the first time in my life.

It was like that, as if someone or something took me into its tenderness, murmuring, *Here, let me help you off with these scratchy, heavy clothes. Look, how there are stones sewn into the hems. How have you carried this weight all your life?*

I resort here to metaphor, knowing no other way to make it clear how everything changed, absolutely changed, absolutely for the better, the best. I did not bring it about. It would be hard to find more convincing evidence that reality is much bigger than our petty notions of control or understanding.

All wanting, all fear, had stopped. There was—there is—a steady stream of joy without cause. No reason, nothing driving it, nothing able to interfere with it. Did I know why this happened? I knew only that I had come home. I knew too, with certainty, that this radical equanimity had been there right along. That it is the nature of us all.

Eventually, I came to understand why I hadn't seen it before, why I hadn't come "home" years sooner, to that place that is the only true beloved. It was because of how I'd been in love with wanting and getting, having and losing. It was because of who I had believed myself to be.

How wrong could a person be?

Open the Door

On the other side of the familiar is the extraordinary.

Have you always known this was so?
That quiet hunch, that there is more?
More to life than the day-to-day absence of satisfaction?

Everything a door, every wall an opening, on second look.
Every floor a trapdoor.
Every solid thing you lean against, a thing on hinges.

When you walk through and look back, it's gone.
When you drop through and look up, there's only sky.
You are floating but nothing's holding you up.

It isn't the way it appears to be.
You aren't what you think you are.

When you think you've got it, and you put your fingers around it,
your hand comes up empty.
There never *was* anything to be afraid of.
Outside the room of every terror,
someone is looking in the window, smiling.
That's you.

Give it a go. You don't have forever.
What if you had only a day in which to do
the one thing that matters?

Today is the day.

Don't try too hard to figure out what this means.
Smell something burning?
It's the inside of your head.

Just let yourself fall backward.
Never mind wondering if you'll be caught.

It isn't a dream.
It's real.
You are the dream.

Know what you know.
Open the door.

The Freedom of Being

Part One

The Lay of the Land

To be conscious is not to be in time.

—T. S. ELIOT

I

The Human Condition

Of human nature, two things can be said:

(1) We are free.

(2) We do not realize it.

Free: able to be in the presence of anything, any condition, and to be unchanged by it. Purely content, at ease. Like an open window, the breeze blowing in and back out again. All of it (everything that happens) comes and goes, even the close-up things, and inside, the stillness does not waver. Free means living as pure awareness—awareness that's only secondarily a person.

What We Don't Know

We are free, and we don't know it. It feels the furthest thing from possible, that it could be so. We'd swear we're at the mercy of what goes wrong, what goes right.

And yet (here is the truth), freedom is right here. So far away, it seems, but right here. Even as you could spend your whole life chasing it down, you have the scent of it on you all the while.

The perfection is right alongside the mess, intimate with the misaligned mini-disaster that life appears to be. Close as the breath that's moving in you right now.

Sometimes you get a whiff of it on the wind. A scrap of a melody playing in the distance, beyond what you're otherwise paying attention to (some useless thing or other).

You could be done with suffering. The thing with no longing, that does not know fear, moves as you move. It asks no act of forgiveness or understanding, nor healing or mastery. It's just here: real as rock, air, dirt. It doesn't await you later. It's not outside you, or in spite of you. You *are* it. It's so close you cannot see it. You look through its eyes at the world around you.

You could let go of what's hobbled you all your life. Something could shift. Let yourself know that it could be otherwise. You think you need to limit yourself with ideas of how-it's-been, what-seems-likely. You don't.

Your essential nature will wait forever for you to notice— you that insist on averting your eyes; you, so full of misplaced longing, managing to invent difficulty, drowning in perpetually unmet desire for something you think will take away the pain. Some flimsy thing.

When this thing seizes you in its teeth and takes you over, when you become *that*, and all the rest of what seemed real is obliterated, then you will look at who-you-were and feel a terrible poignancy. Such pointless aching.

See how a mother lion carries her young. How she grasps the skin at the back of its neck with her glistening teeth that slaughter, how she holds it and will not let go? This is how it is. This is what attends you.

Once you see, you're shocked to discover it was here all along. That all the while you looked for it, you'd been pushing it to the side so you could look behind it to see if you could find it.

Somebody who tells the truth about this doesn't do it expecting that now it will become perfectly obvious that you already have what you're looking for. (We'd all wish for it to work that way.)

No, when someone tells the truth, it's so you'll stop looking elsewhere than the sound of your pulse in your ears, the crash of a dish hitting the floor.

And for goodness sake, don't expect to find it in the grave.

The news that it's as close as the taste of the inside of your own mouth is supposed to be encouraging. Stop expecting to find it out there. Elsewhere, later. It *is* the looker. It *is* the looking.

Do you think these are just words chasing their own tails?

Discovering the truth about yourself is like cutting yourself for the first time, encountering that sticky red, and realizing it was there all the time. Put your tongue to it. Taste it.

To one longing to know the delicious freedom, it seems this state must be on the other side of the world, lifetimes away. People talk themselves into the idea that it's remote, can never be gotten to, because they know how seldom it's realized, put on and worn, like a garment. It must be hard to find, or else more would.

Being told this reality is in plain sight can be perfectly maddening. To want the luxury of it, to be told it's possible—to hear it's underneath your skin—yet you cannot touch it.

But there it is.

Why would one who knows lie about this? Would a story about great distance be consoling?

Hearing of the exquisite proximity doesn't mean you automatically get to feel it in your fingers. Just because it doesn't happen on your schedule of wanting doesn't mean it isn't here.

It is, you see, a matter of perspective. The fact doesn't change. It's the *looking* that changes. Once you see, you realize truth always was just on the other side of a tissue-paper wall, dying for a rupture, a flame.

All the Same

Another thing that can be said about human nature is that we're all alike. (What mental static *that* starts up.)

We're the same as one another, on the level of each of our "selves": the conditioned, egoic one, as well as the self that's awake, free, condition-less.

As formless essence, each person (indeed, all of existence) is pure, undifferentiated *being*. Awakened presence doesn't experience identity or imperfection.

Not everyone encountering this idea will believe it to be true. Many will dismiss it as wishful thinking. Even spiritual seekers (supposed to "know better") may find it hard to believe they already are what they seek.

Still, the notion that causeless joy is universally innate is doubtlessly pleasing. What's not so welcome is the idea that we're also essentially indistinct on the level of our familiar selves.

How the ego (convinced of its uniqueness and value) balks at this proposition. Yet we are universally susceptible to conditioning. We believe we *are* what the mind says we are. We're all subject to our given circumstances, prone to identify with our thoughts, protective of our (quirkily unique) egoic selves.

We also share a constitutional ignorance of our essential freedom.

For a seeker of the truth, what's worthier of attention than a person's distinguishing features (vastly more) is our existential *sameness*. Which is to say, the human condition.

No matter the apparent differences, all (alas) are in the same boat. The sooner you shift attention from the particulars (as if they were the problem) and onto the overwhelming impression that your thoughts are reliable indicators of reality, the sooner something significant can change.

2

How We Tick

Spiritual inquiry has its birth in the longing to know what you are. Who is in this skin? Who is living this life?

When awakening to the truth of being takes place, the revelation isn't intellectual so much as visceral. Nor—if the awakening is radical—is the revelation fleeting. There's a living, sustained knowing of your essential nature, beyond the narrow confines of the egoic self.

The reason ultimate self-knowledge is rare is that virtually all human beings are convinced of the absolute reality of their egoic selves. Although spiritual seekers "know better," the knowing exists on the mental level only, with the exception of infrequent, fleeting glimpses of the higher reality of their nature. Once full awakening has taken place, there is no more doubt or confusion about the nature of the self. Reality is seen for what it is.

Two Selves

In ordinary life, people (including seekers) generally carry on as if they know quite well who they are (as well as who others close to them are) and don't question this assumption except in rare moments of reflection. The self each of us appears to be is the one that's recognizable (by others and over time), having a certain appearance, gender, and name; carrying a collection of memories and beliefs; playing certain roles (familial, social, work-related); having a personality (opinions, quirks, gifts, liabilities). This is the familiar egoic self, the persona around which a person's life is felt to revolve. This is the person affected by experience. This self derives its own definition, and determines its general orientation to life, from what the egoic mind learns and incorporates as true.

All the while that this self is living as though it's the whole story of *who I am*, there's another "self" present (if quietly concealed) within each human being. It isn't subject to the forces that constantly push and pull at the familiar self. It was never uplifted by praise. It never was wounded, had its heart broken, its feelings hurt. It has nothing to process or recover from. It wants nothing. This self is not conditioned by experience, or in any way at the mercy of changeable outer reality. This isn't because it's at a distance from that reality; this "higher" self is, in fact, entirely aware of and comfortable with whatever is. Indeed, it does not experience itself as *apart from* reality.

The presence of the "more real" self within goes largely unrecognized by the vast majority of human beings. Among those few who sense its presence—who make an effort to reach it, aspiring to live *as* it (rather than as the familiar self)—even they experience precious few moments as though they *are* that profoundly peaceful being. For the most part, they resign themselves to taking on faith that it's within, real, awaiting revelation.

In this discussion, continuing reference will be made to the presence of two selves. One will be referred to as the familiar or egoic self, the ego-mind, and the apparent or conditioned self. The other will be called the higher or real self, or the deep truth of human nature.

Two caveats are in order.

First, the two "selves" are not literally distinct entities within a human being, although it's convenient to talk about them as though they were. They do *feel* noticeably different from one another. In a given episode, the difference between the vantage point of the familiar self and that of the higher self is so dramatic that it can seem as though there are, in fact, two distinct people here. For most individuals who awaken, so pronounced is the contrast between before and after that it's as though one person has died and another has been born. But these bits of evidence suggestive of a dual nature are only perceptual flukes occasioned by the limitations of the mind. They tell us all we need to know about the ego's power to convince us of its authority.

The second point has to do with the degree of *reality* of each self. The "lesser" or apparent reality of the familiar self, by contrast with the absolute reality of the higher self, is a *relative* matter. The self you appear to be is in some sense "real," if only in a practical way. Indeed, the higher self is no "self" at all, being utterly devoid of anything personal or particular (even while it experiences itself, and all around it, from within the "container" of awareness of an individual person).

In the contemporary environment of nondual spiritual teachings, it's worth looking at the widespread insistence that "no one is here." To someone absorbed in the apparent reality of the familiar self, saying that *no one is here* accomplishes nothing. Someone does *seem* to be here. Until you directly experience the oneness of all, it's a mental construct of no use. Moreover, while it may be "true" that from the perspective of absolute freedom, there's only unity (or perhaps nothing at all), since even an awakened life is lived largely on this material plane, it's convenient to carry on as though there *is* someone here—as though there are, in fact, a lot of someones here.

A way to account for the apparent coexistence of two selves is that the higher self, being unconstrained by the limitations the lower self is subject to, experiences a higher order of reality. The familiar self (like all of the observable world) is a form existing *within* that reality. *From within the world of form*, the apparent self is real (as real as any other form).

The point of awakening is to experience life *as the embodiment* of That—the unmanifest perfection *in the form of* a human being. Even as you're aware that the reality of the apparent self is relative only.

But these are just words. From the point of view of the familiar self, they accomplish little; to liberated awareness, they're unnecessary.

The One Doing the Knowing

By what means is the higher self known?

As the spiritual life develops, there's a growing sense of the presence of more than one *knower* within. It becomes apparent that more than one kind of intelligence is available to a self-aware person. There's a sense of multiple possibilities in the approach to a moment or a thought.

There's more than one way to see. There's more than one "place" to look from.

One who's aware of being two "selves" has realized this by having *experienced* the two ways of knowing, of seeing. Because the feeling state of each is conspicuous, there's compelling evidence that there's "more than one of me."

The familiar "knower" is ordinary consciousness, which takes place within the confines of the thought-conditioned mind. Understanding occurs within a framework relative to yourself (your circumstances, identity, beliefs, issues). This knower is mental/emotional in nature. The one doing the knowing and the knowing itself are egoic phenomena.

The other kind of intelligence lives outside the confines of the conditioned self. Still, there's the felt presence of a *someone* here, a living intelligence able to direct itself to a particular thing—to focus awareness, to pay attention. To see, to know. It's able to purely *look*, without bias, agenda, self-interest, or discomfort. This higher knowing carries a sensation of alert vitality.

Where is each "self" felt to be, when you experience it as being what you are? The one exists in the realm of thought and emotion, in the eyes of others, in time. It's at a distance from reality. The other (the *real* self) comes to be known in the present encounter with reality, in attention unmediated by thought or resistance. This self is not felt to be separate from what-is.

When the Familiar Self Sees

From the perspective of the person completely convinced of the substance and reality of the egoic self, there's only one way to see, one place to look from: through the eyes of the self conditioned by experience, the mind-encased self that experiences itself as a continuity over time. This self is solid and significant. Whatever is seen is processed in terms of it; all experience is in some way *about* it.

This persona is profoundly self-centered. Even if it's concerned for others' well-being, even if it's self-effacing, or self-loathing, this is the case. The egoic self is felt to be the center of an ever-moving world: moving through space, moving through time. What "moves" is a roughly stable entity (recognizable day-to-day) consisting of a body of memory, a certain disposition (personality, appearance, desires, fears), and a compelling interest in maintaining itself. Its highest priority is to keep itself going.

When this self looks, when it experiences life, it sees *through* (as a lens) the accumulation of its conditioned mental and emotional processors. This self—the familiar person each of us seems to be—processes whatever happens in terms of prior learning about its own identity, how life works, who other people are.

For the great part of humanity, this is all there is to a person (self as well as others). It's the sole experiencer of meaning, of fulfillment (or its absence). It seems to be the only "place" to look from, the only available awareness. A human being appears to be a single self—exotically complicated, and in no way harmonious in its parts, but nevertheless integrated in some sense. It may change over time, and may appear ultimately unsatisfying, but it's felt to be all there is.

When Awakeness Sees

The person who's awakened (a tiny fraction of humanity) has that same self, with two conspicuous differences. It's not taken very seriously (one's own or another's), and it's felt to exist within a soft, larger, depersonalized awareness. The egoic self is known to be no legitimate indicator of reality, but is just a "way of being in the world." It's a convenient construct, a means of being with other people, of getting things done, enjoying. Its reality is seen as *relative*, whereas for the vast majority of humankind, its reality is experienced as absolute.

The egoic self, because it's a closed system (unable to see beyond its self-defined world), is not equipped to "understand" awakeness. Because ego exists as a form within the higher reality, however, awakeness *is* able to fathom the familiar self, in a way the latter cannot hope to see itself. The ego is entirely transparent to the higher self.

The intelligence of the higher "self" differs from that available to the familiar self, which is subject to bias, to ceaseless, ravenous self-aggrandizement. The non-egoic awareness is able to "look" without its own interest at heart. It doesn't *have* self-interest. It doesn't perceive itself as being subject to harm nor even to change, so it doesn't need attention or maintenance. It doesn't look for meaning, for fulfillment or security.

Whatever is seen is not in service to the psychologically understood "self." What's happening isn't felt to be about you, but simply *is*. In this mode of being, the familiar self is often felt literally to dissolve—or, if there's awareness of its presence, it appears to be a made-up thing (rather like a thought).

By what means, then, is the higher self to be known? It's knowable *by itself;* that is, it cannot be known via the egoic self. When deep nature is being experienced, it's being sensed from within itself. Knower and known are one.

When you're aware of the higher self, it's because you *are* it. You're looking around at yourself, from within yourself—your higher self, that is.

Going Back and Forth ("Losing It")

For someone having (as it were) one foot in each world, a person seeking to discover the truth of human nature, there's an awareness of these two "selves." The aim of the spiritual journey is to experience more of life as the higher self—to live as though you *are* empty awareness, and only incidentally the egoic self.

Most of the time, even for the ardent seeker, the familiar self continues to have the more compelling reality. The more real it seems, the less real the other "self" is felt to be, to be "seen from." During the predominating times that the ego holds sway, there's a sense that the true self "goes away."

Meanwhile, the awakened person never forgets that the familiar self is a thought-up thing, a persona adopted for the sake of practicality. This pretense is known to be the universal human condition (however seldom individuals realize this about themselves).

Even individuals not intent on self-knowledge, locked within the determined impression that they *are* their apparent selves, may report having glimpsed a different reality, a charged moment when life felt conspicuously different from the usual. This tends to be seen as a fluke, an oddity of perception. It came and went.

"It" didn't go away. It only appeared to because of the return to the compelling reality of the familiar.

Given the ongoing presence of the two "selves," the possibility is ongoing that the utterly free one can be discovered. The potential is constantly alive that the true self could be assumed as one's dominant reality.

The awake state isn't something a person evolves into *over time*, nor is it granted from without. Awakening is a matter of perceiving what already *is*. It asks not an actual change so much as a perspective shift. This is why it's said *you are already free; you just don't know it*. The whole task of the spiritual journey is to discover that all along you've been where you've been trying to get.

Time and the Mind

The impression that a person *is* the ego is sustained by the apparent reality of time. A human being appears to be a continuity flowing through time, which appears to be a medium. The egoic self does such things as process and recall, reviewing life-so-far and pronouncing it satisfying or unfulfilled. There appears to be a roughly stable entity over the succession of moments that constitute a life. A person does change, physically and otherwise; life experience has its effect. But when the mind looks at the past, or projects to what's ahead, there's a clear impression of ongoingness-of-self.

Returning the favor, the apparent continuity of the familiar self (like the ongoingness of the physical world) supports the impression that time has an objective reality—that is, an existence independent of the mind's grasp of events that take place in time. We depend for many things on the assumption that time is real. A historical review of events couldn't make sense without time; the phenomenon of change, the observation of linearity, causation, order—all depend upon a before and an after, a succession. We need to enter into the world of time in order to plan. Looking at the evolution of a species, at the changes in the earth's geology, it's clear that things take place over time. People and houses age over time. It takes time to get from one place to another.

Yet life as it's actually experienced occurs only *now*. A succession of moments—what looks to the mind like a flow—is really one now followed by another. Each thing takes place in a particular moment, in *some* present. Once a moment has passed, whatever took place is recoverable only via the mind. The evident "series" quality of our existence appears only when intelligent awareness tries to make coherence of what's actually one stillness followed by another. The compelling appearance of movement has no corresponding objective reality.

It's like an old-fashioned motion-picture film that's actually a series of stills, the projector moving the film fast enough to create the illusion of motion. The mind (ever in pursuit of meaning) does this same thing with the recollected series of stills, giving the impression of motion—what we insist upon defining as "life." But the actual experience of a moment of life as it's happening is a stillness.

Similarly, the continuous entity that you appear to be, over time, exists only when you *think* about it—that is, when you reflect on yourself, on your life, looking at the before and the after of experiences.

The highly evolved human mind is able to picture past moments and projected future ones in such vivid detail that it's as though an event in some other time is real *now*—of the same order of reality as the actual present moment of life. Being the inventor of time, the mind deftly convinces itself (with the ego going along for the ride) that whatever it brings into focus via thought is real. Even if the thing took place a long time ago, or hasn't happened yet, it's absorbing attention *now*, which fools the egoic mind and emotions into "experiencing" something that isn't actually happening.

The ability to remember and anticipate is akin to the mind's capacity to picture what's *spatially* remote—on (say) the other side of the world, or inside your body. Just as the mind is able to imagine something that isn't actually happening now, it's able to envision a thing that's happening now but not *here*. So it's possible to "know," to visualize, that something many miles away is in progress, even though you're not there to witness it. As long as you're thinking about it, it can be as absorbing of attention as something right here.

That we can picture something distant in place or time, summoning it in awareness *as though it were real here and now*, is a capacity particular to humankind, one verging on miraculous. This ability to envision what's not present is doubtless one of the blessings of our condition. It enables us to plan, to provide for possibilities and likelihoods. It enables us to learn, to review what's happened and draw conclusions that may favorably affect what's to come.

The mind's power also has everything to do with why our familiar selves seem so enduringly real, so truly who we appear to be. And how we can manage to stay so caught up in their impression of reality that we're never able to discover what we *really* are, beyond our mentally constructed selves—to experience presence moment to moment, to live as free beings.

Ceaseless mental activity is able to carry on because the mind manages to convince us of the reality of its contents. Most mental activity is focused on something that's not here and now. It's because the mind is so good at approximating reality that the present fills up with things that aren't immediately real. Belief in time enables us to worry, regret, hope, and live in the past, such that thoughts often absorb all our attention. There's no end of apparently valid content for the mind. Attention to present reality is thereby eclipsed, pretty constantly, by mental activity. Higher awareness (beyond the mind) has no "space" in which its presence may be known, and the present—the only "piece" of life that's real—goes by unnoticed, unlived.

When life is seen as that constantly moving strip of film, whose motion inside the remembering, projecting mind is so compelling, what happens? A person comes to the end of life and cannot shake the feeling of having missed it. The standard explanation for that lamentable realization is that you didn't *spend your time* doing what you'd have most liked to. That is, filling your allotted time with the most valued content. But that isn't really why life was missed. It's because life was spent by "living" in the head. How we spend time doesn't matter nearly so much as what's going on with the attention while we're doing it. Strange, perhaps . . . not what we expect . . . but nevertheless true.

Life is not really a strip of fast-moving film. That phenomenon is artificial, mind-made. Life is *this moment*.

Seeing how belief in time interferes with present-moment awareness leads back to the question *Who am I?* The higher self senses itself in a singular moment of presence—*not* over time. In a moment of awakeness, you sense the presence that's independent of mind, ego, time. There's a feeling of vitality, attention that's utterly still, without any urging toward the next moment or toward mental commentary.

The familiar self senses nothing outside itself, having access only to its self-made container of thoughts, which lives (a poor approximation of "life") in time. While the higher self experiences only the present moment as real, the familiar self lives as though the recollected past and the anticipated future were as real as the *now*.

A person absorbed in ego can't necessarily step beyond the familiar self, just by wishing to do so, and assume the perspective of the higher self. But a person *can* realize—if the attention is sufficient—that the impression of self, in a given moment, is entirely determined by the ego-mind. By that simple recognition, each moment carries the potential that the higher presence will be sensed. Believing it's necessary to wait for enlightenment to reveal the truth is allowing an idea of a future possibility to deflect attention from what's already here now.

Language

The mind's ability to picture something remote in time or place and pronounce it real is supported by language. The name for a thing functions as a placeholder for the thing itself. The word becomes fastened to it. If you know the bird you're hearing or seeing is called a chickadee, it's unlikely you'll encounter that type of bird without its name being somewhere around the edges of your auditory/visual perception.

We use language to impose order on chaos, to assemble stories about experience that will enable us to learn, to control forces and predict developments, to relay information. As soon as a story is told about an event, as soon as a thing is labeled, the word-rendering assumes a certain authority. The more a story is told, the more objectively accurate the given rendering appears. A twice-told story takes on a life of its own, yielding only reluctantly to accommodate any newly acquired information.

Having a name confers a measure of mastery over a thing. Adam's naming of the animals gave him dominion over them. One person's description of a piece of reality often differs radically from another's. The power of language to define is how one people can justify subjugating another. Why feminism made such a big deal over a married woman's right to retain her own name. How whole histories written about a single event can be so diverse, each having the ring of truth.

So convincingly does a word stand in for reality that it can elicit a visceral fight-or-flight response to a danger that's not actual. If someone calls out *Fire!*, your mental, emotional, and physical response has almost the same force as if you'd seen the flames yourself (and it's the same even if it turns out nothing's burning).

While language usefully assists efforts to improve our world, it also enables us to distance ourselves from reality, *without necessarily realizing that is happening.* Words carry the power to manipulate behavior, to move a person to do something otherwise unthinkable. In the absence of critical thinking, it's possible to fail to realize there's latitude in what to call a phenomenon—that is, how to think of it. Once you've accepted the "accuracy" of the name of a thing, believing the chosen language completely accounts for its truth, and the identification of name-with-thing has been established, you're living within a reality that's defined by what it's called. When you pronounce a thing *good* or *bad*, it *becomes* that, as if objectively. If you're managing a war, *collateral damage* is a handy name for the unintended death of civilians, because it puts distance between the uncomfortable truth and anyone using or hearing the expression. Change what a thing is called, and you change how it's perceived.

Convinced as we are that language reliably embodies a phenomenon, we mistake a name for the thing itself. The result (since language is of the mind) is that we live much of life in the head.

The power of words to mediate reality is one way the self-referential world of the ego-mind is maintained. Individuals create their own reality (including their sense of themselves) and *solidify* that creation via language. *I am a* patriot. *I am a* teacher. *I am an* alcoholic. Language helps us construct self-defining "boxes" around ourselves, giving us prescription-lens windows to look through, conscribing our ability to directly encounter the moment.

Presence and Timelessness

A hallmark of the awakened state (whether it's enduring or fleeting) is purity of attention to the immediate. The word "presence" as truly describes the awake condition as anything could, because it conveys how the perceiving, living intelligence is *present with* the *present* moment. Awakened awareness is literally all-of-a-piece with the present reality being perceived. The one being present and the reality being encountered are experienced as a whole.

Anytime you're in a state of pure attentiveness, focused entirely on something that's happening now, you don't feel at a distance from what-is. There's no sense of being an entity observing something, existing in time. You *are* the moment.

This phenomenon is sometimes inexactly referred to as *being one with* something, or having merged with it. But the actual experience is of *identity* with the moment. In the aliveness of presence, no *merging* is felt, because there's no separate someone having an experience. There is simply *happening*, simply *this*, whenever attention is given fully to whatever's happening.

This attention can feel its aliveness only in the present. Reality is a feature of *this moment*—not of some recalled or anticipated moment, or period of time (last winter, the year you were eighteen, all day yesterday).

When you experience pure attention, in a moment when you're riveted on some present happening—something overwhelmingly beautiful, dangerous, bizarre, painful, shocking—time appears to stop. A musical performance of extraordinary beauty, the sheer face of a mountain being ascended, someone in the room having a heart attack—at such a moment, attention is undiluted by anything in the mind. You're stunned into momentary awakeness, though the "content" of the present may be in no way "spiritual" or even necessarily pleasant. The essential feature is purity of attention. Such a moment often will be recalled later as having a quality of conspicuous stillness, mental quietude, and vitality—*even if the moment carried difficult content.*

The impression of time having "stopped" is just an appearance. It's not that time was flowing and now has paused. *It never was in motion.* It's just that at a moment of pure attention, the profound stillness within is fleetingly realized. The flood of peace and well-being comes because the mind has grown quiet. It's stopped insisting that words and thoughts are reality. The mind isn't *thinking* about what's happening. It's not narrating, labeling, anticipating what's next. It has dropped the pretense that anything but *now* is real.

Such is the power of attention.

The exquisite stillness outside of the illusion of time is the experience of eternity. Eternity isn't an unending succession of moments, stretching into some unimaginable forever. It is timelessness. In absolute presence, this is known.

The present moment isn't located *between* the past and the future, however much the mind might wish to insist on this picture of time. The now isn't a point where past and future meet. The now is outside of time altogether. Time has no independent existence outside of the mind looking before and after. Other moments can occur only as thoughts, not as inhabitable reality.

The higher awareness knows that only *this moment* is real, that the future will never come. Maddened by this idea, the mind cannot comprehend its truth.

The reason an awake person doesn't fear death (which seems to exist "in the future") isn't because of some assurance of afterlife or otherworldliness. It's because what's not immediate isn't experienced as real. What's not real cannot be perceived as a threat. It's understood that death will someday come. It just isn't relevant now. When the now of dying comes, then it will be real—and if you're awake, you won't think to resist it. You'll simply be with the moments leading up to death, as you've been with all previous moments.

The other reason death isn't feared is that the body is no longer identified with as being *you*.

Life Is Now

All of rememberable life is just a thought (however significant it was at the time, however enduring its impact). Only in the present-tense moment it occurred would it ever be real. Anything anticipated, when (if) it happens, will happen in *some* moment. It will be real then, and then only.

What's crucial, for the person engaged in spiritual inquiry, is to get the difference between the "life" of a moment *remembered* now, and the *actual* life of that moment, as it was lived. *To not confuse the one with the other.* If you ate a bowl of oatmeal this morning, it was reality then. Now, it's a thought. The memory is a (real) mental construct. But it's not the same kind of real as the bowl of oatmeal was when it was being eaten.

It's not that you have to convince yourself that time "isn't real." It's that whenever you're thinking about something in another time (or place), realize its *sole* reality is the form of a thought. When you confuse memory (or any thought) with reality, you miss the now.

The familiar self experiences the mind's contents as being of the same order of reality as what's actually taking place here and now. This self has a pretty constant need for content, and the mind happily obliges. Over and over again, life is happening *here* but attention is elsewhere. The goal is to learn not to confuse a mental construct (however useful it may be) with reality. There's nothing wrong with mentally evoking the picture of another time or place, so long as you realize the thought has no independent reality. As soon as you stop thinking the thought, whatever it points to ceases to be.

From within higher awareness, when the mind is being rightly used, there can be deliberate mental reference to something beyond the immediate scene. But there's no illusion that it's real.

Either you're living life, or you're "living" in the facsimile of reality that your mind creates moment to moment. You don't have to *make yourself* be in the now. There's no trick to make yourself be in the present. You already *are*. There's no place else you could be. You have only to notice what's already the case.

How much do you want to have your life—to really have it, to *be* it? To come to your last moment and know that life didn't pass you by? It isn't life's "content" that determines its value. It's the *awareness* you bring to it, moment to moment. It's attention itself. Presence is its same self regardless of the particulars of the moment.

3

Potential and Fulfillment

What does it mean to have a good life, to achieve your potential as a human being? What constitutes success? What does it mean to reach maturity? And how does any of it relate to awakening?

The specifics vary with the individual, of course, but in general, fulfillment is thought to come of realizing your potential in mind, heart, and body. In a successful life, at least some of your dreams reach fruition, perhaps resulting in outer signs of effectiveness, worthy of respect and admiration.

A good life, as it's commonly understood, comes of applying your innate gifts to undertakings of value to yourself and others. You enjoy yourself, and you have fulfilling relationships. There's a healthy self-image and a solid identity built on clear values and beliefs, which are reflected in your work and personal life. You meet your obligations and assume responsibility for your actions. Where you see improvements that could be made to yourself or your environment, you make earnest efforts in those directions. The world is better for having had you in it.

A Well-Developed Self

The messages and role models promoted in youth, continuing into adulthood and through maturity, encourage the pursuit of personal qualities and behavior that will enhance the familiar self. That's where the focus is: on developing and expressing a well-defined identity. You're encouraged to cultivate a sturdy sense of self, to distinguish yourself from others, to know what you believe in, to take pride in what you do—all so you can feel good about who you are.

Look at your own life (past and current). Where have your energy and time been invested? What has your training been? When you've felt happy or unhappy, successful or disappointed, mature or embarrassingly naive, hasn't it usually been related to things of the egoic self?

When are young people—in families or schools, or even religious institutions—encouraged to explore the higher consciousness? To become alert to that inner knowing that doesn't waver in the face of life experience? Where are there messages inviting a person at any stage of life to seek truth within, without reference to the inherited cultural legacy? Who ever says the best thing you could do is discover the innate presence that's not prey to fear, resistance, or the desire for control? You will look in vain, in the world at large, for encouragement to pursue the underlying reality.

Yet it's stunning how the focus on the familiar self fades to nothingness when a person makes the shocked discovery of truth that halts the machinery of ego, bringing blessed quietude to the mind and flooding awareness with clarity.

The messages we're given, beginning in youth, are counter to all that's discovered in awakened presence. Consider what we're taught:

We Are Taught	We Are **Not** Taught
It's important to be well thought of, and it's good to love yourself, to have a healthy ego, solid self-esteem.	The egoic self is a mind-invented construct and the cause of suffering.
It's good to have a clear sense of who you are.	Your appearance of being an individual is minor in the larger scheme of reality. In a life of ultimate value, there's no identification with *anything*.
You *are* your body, your good name, your history, your heritage, your work, your roles, your relationships.	You are formless emptiness.
You should be willing to take a stand for what you believe in.	There's no such thing as a "true" belief; all belief is mind-limited and ego-nurturing, and it blocks access to the truth.
It's the way time is spent—the content of a life, a moment—that matters.	Awareness is what matters.
Having more time means potential for more good things to happen—achievement, healing, finding love, learning.	Only this moment is real; the future will never come.
Security is worth working for and can be attained.	There's no such thing as security, nor do you need it to be at peace.
Love is something given to another; gotten from another; love is earned, nearly always conditional, and can change to hatred.	Love is unconditional, omnipresent, the nature of existence.
Evil and suffering must be resisted if change for the better is to happen.	Nonresistance—because of its attunement to reality—is the environment in which change becomes possible.
It's best not to dwell in uncomfortable feelings, like grief and anger; better to turn from them, in favor of positive feelings and "good" behavior.	Whatever is must be allowed, because it's real.
Delight and satisfaction are *earned* commodities. They must be worked for, deserved (or not).	At the core of every human being is a causeless joy and equanimity.
A successful, fulfilled life has to do with outer achievements and inner character traits.	Fulfillment is knowing formless stillness.
The name of the game is to keep improving yourself.	If you want to be free, you must be willing to lose yourself.

A person who wants to awaken to deeper nature is being asked, essentially, to question all that's normally valued, that's supposed to define a worthwhile life. We are, in short, at odds with ourselves. Is it any wonder awakening is so rare? Considering all the effort given to bolstering the ego—the emphasis on self-esteem, reputation, achievement, physical appearance, material acquisition—it's a miracle awakening ever happens at all.

Is There More to Life?

It's natural, every so often, to assess how it's going so far in this thing called life. Some kind of standard for success is carried around inside most people's heads, having to do with what they want for themselves, what they've been told they ought to aspire to, and so on. Anyone who grows up in the modern western culture is well acquainted, by the end of adolescence, with the pressure to get it all sorted out, to get going. The mid-life crisis and the death bed are classic settings for self-review, as is any major crisis or turning-point. Many people, in moments of private reflection, lament that they haven't done very well—at least, not as well as they could have, or thought they might.

Having arrived someplace significant and looking around the new terrain, a person may wonder in the quiet of the middle of the night, *Is this what it was all supposed to be about?*

Those individuals who've accomplished impressive things, who seem to have reached their potential, attaining fulfillment others only dream of—even they will sometimes admit to an underlying angst. They look at all they've done and think, *Shouldn't there be more to life?* There's a sense that something is missing. There's a longing to know—to occupy—a state that's not dependent on continuing success.

For some, in the aftermath of the height of achievement comes a malaise, even a despair. No matter what has been attained, there's an awareness that it's subject to threat, to change—that there may be a fall from the height. Anyone of reasonable intelligence and experience knows that nothing is certain. When the fall comes, if it does, the devastation to one's sense of self can be terrible. Even if it never comes, in the background of awareness lives the knowledge that it *could*. On the level of the familiar self, in the shadow of every attainment lurks some measure of insecurity, a subtle dread, a practiced denial.

It's in these dread-filled shadows—or in the actualization of some awful loss or undermining—that the spiritual life may find its birth. Challenge to the realm of the egoic self is often the setting where the life-altering question comes to flower: *Isn't there something, some reality, that's not subject to threat, that's of a value beyond all of this that's seemed to matter so much?*

It's not that what high achievers have accomplished isn't *relatively* valuable. It's just that the realization of the narrowly defined self—however impressive—doesn't tell the whole story of the potential of a human life. It's not that a person shouldn't bother with the things society says to value. It's just that they do not—they *cannot*—satisfy the deep hunger to know what a life is ultimately about.

Whatever gives rise to pride and admiration necessarily plays itself out in the arena of the egoic self. However successfully developed the ego, it cannot fail to be hobbled by its nature as a self-serving entity: because its primary wish is to keep itself going (having no incentive or ability to look for meaning outside its self-defined world), the ego will inevitably be subject to undermining, and therefore to conservatism and fear.

Isn't there something within that's precious, in and of itself? Something in us senses that it is so, or wishes it were.

Two Ways of Looking at Human Potential

If you look at the full picture of the makeup of a human being, taking into account not only the familiar self but also the higher awareness that "contains" the ego and coexists with it, the possibility for fulfillment goes well beyond what's ordinarily defined as human potential.

Which is not to say that spiritual realization is a natural or logical next step beyond the attainment of a satisfying egoic self. It would be a mistake to see liberation as the final frontier for a highly successful person, as if it were on a trajectory in common with familiar achievement. Ordinary attainment is no foundation for reaching what's beyond all limitation. A person who's succeeded in world-defined terms and now (having no place left to go) seeks to become established in presence, will be dismayed by the necessity to jettison the very thing all the attention has been lavished on: the well-polished, high-functioning ego.

Occasionally, awakening will come to a person who's achieved great things, someone accustomed to admiration and emulation. Such a person will report that all the previous satisfaction and recognition have dissolved into insignificance. The solid identity has fallen apart into nothingness. Radical fulfillment is the end of any of it mattering.

The familiar kind of human development does not naturally prepare a person for radical fulfillment (except insofar as it provides the setup for its own undermining, the devastation of ego occasionally resulting in awakening). Having its own well-being as its primary focus, the ego is simply not equipped to take a person beyond itself.

Since awakening involves ceasing to take seriously the ordinary self, it may be that the last thing a well-developed, high-achieving individual would desire is spiritual liberation. A person who's done well in life, in society's terms, is in for a big surprise, if spiritual opening begins to happen. After a lifelong focus on self-enhancement, the identity begins to thin out, to soften. With growing spiritual maturity, what's seen is that the "thinner" the conditioned self, the more possible it is to sense the higher presence within.

The fulfillment of the conditioned self involves an accumulation of knowledge and experience, the maturing of an identity—things that take place *over time*. It asks a certain vigilance to maintain itself. Radical fulfillment, by contrast, removes all consideration of temporal experience. The realization of the higher self takes place *outside* of time, in moments of utter stillness. Sensing its own vastly greater reality, the "self" discovered in awakened presence cares nothing for concerns of the ego. Awakeness asks no vigilance.

A person's intellect and creativity may be impressively developed, relationships deeply satisfying, the facets of the personality well-integrated. Yet even with maturity in these arenas, until the higher self is known, an individual has realized only the relative youthfulness of what's possible for a human life. From the vantage point of the potential for awakened awareness, even the most deeply fulfilled life as an egoic self amounts to perpetual adolescence.

Only with the dissolving of the familiar self does true maturity become possible.

4

A New Orientation to Life

The day you discover you're in prison (and have been, all your life) is a great day.

It's the day you acknowledge that you're not going to find ultimate fulfillment and well-being in the promised places. It's when you see that the feel of life has less to do with the outer situation and much more to do with your experience of it. Only (as you are now seeing) your ego-mind seems to be in charge of that. Hence, the prison.

You could say it's a dark day. But no: a whole new world just opened to you.

Until that day comes, you've been like everybody else on the planet: trying to find happiness by improving yourself and your circumstances. You've believed that what's between you and joy is whatever seems to be wrong with you or your life. So your attention has gone there—to *fixing* things. Over and over again, you've used this method, for decades probably. Trying to manage the things that make up the content of your life. Reacting to events in a way that will improve your situation, or at least not make it any worse. You've found this approach works intermittently, although only occasionally achieving a satisfaction that runs deep . . . but even then, it almost never lasts. Life, you've come to see, is a roller coaster of success and failure, ease and struggle, delight and misery. That seems to be the way of things, and reaching maturity amounts, in part, to having made your peace with a life that can never be ultimately satisfying.

The majority of humanity stays on the roller coaster all the way to the grave, hoping over and over again that the next high point will hold.

You, on the other hand, have seen something.

The Birth of a Seeker

When you're fortunate, something happens to shake your faith in the approach to life that you've taken thus far. Something causes you to shift your eyes from whatever they've fixated on to your own interior. Maybe a crisis sets you back hard, or you're simply weary of the cycle of hope and disappointment. Perhaps you intuit that there's more to you, more to life. Maybe you've had the sense of a something-deeper for years, but haven't given it real attention. Now, after a long time of pursuing other routes to fruition, you're turning toward the rich silence whose presence you sense within.

But when you go looking for that stillness, you can hardly find it for all the racket in your mind. The fact that you suffer, that equanimity eludes you, seems increasingly to point to the activity of the ego-serving mind, with its power to color your experience of reality. The more attention you pay to the interior of your head, the more you begin to realize (if you're lucky, and brave) that what's eluded you really cannot be blamed on how things are going in your outer life. The longed-for peace and contentment, you're sensing, is not to be found *out there* anywhere. The focus of attention is broadening to take in not only what happens in life, but also what your mind makes of it.

When awareness shifts to the inner life—when you realize to what extent the ego-mind is running the show—you've come to where suffering has some hope of abating. This realization has the potential to bring you to a place where all longing dissolves into presence. Which is why it's a great day when you discover your imprisonment.

Before It Gets Better, It Gets Worse

Meanwhile, seeing how it all works can make you a little crazy. Because understanding the power of the mind to imprison does not mean you're automatically able to get free of it. The growing ability to see yourself more truthfully is a potent catalyst for change . . . but it's not necessarily a lot of fun.

As your self-awareness deepens, as you become more subtly attuned to your interior, you become intimate with this prison you inhabit. You see how trapped you are in what your mind makes of reality, how much your emotional state is controlled by stories you tell yourself. You get a sense of the overwhelming momentum of your history, how you've been conditioned by experience, how your beliefs were formed. You see how convincingly it all defines you. You see the extent to which you identify with what you do, your background, your physical features.

It's clear you didn't land in this morass by some kind of bad luck, or because someone wished you a miserable life. Gradually, it dawns that you've actually *built* the prison you dwell in. Not only did you construct it, but in fact *you work hard every day to maintain it.* The very thing that causes all the trouble— that's between you and freedom—is the object of an enormous amount of devoted (if unconscious) attention.

The recognition of this truth can be devastating.

Still, it's a great place to have come to—the willingness to acknowledge and to confront your own complicity in your suffering. Because it's the seed of radical change.

Most people never make the discovery that they live their lives in a prison of their own making. Never forget that *simply seeing the location and the severity of the problem* puts you in a tiny and fortunate segment of humankind.

You want things to be better for yourself, and even if you can't quite see yet how to bring that about, at least you intuit that such a thing is possible. Perhaps you sense that you already carry within yourself that which you seek.

Starting on the Spiritual Journey

The pull to the inner life has launched you on a spiritual journey. Because you're willing to look at yourself in fresh and courageous ways, you're equipped as you were not before to loosen the hold on established patterns of identity and reactivity, with the potential for a real reduction in suffering.

As you set out on this journey of self-discovery, you may naturally gravitate toward others who are similarly inclined. It can feel like coming home to spend time in the company of like-minded seekers earnestly practicing inquiry. A spiritual discipline or path may appeal to you as a context for keeping focused on the inner life. Perhaps you're drawn to a meditation practice, or moved by a book or a body of teachings that illuminates the workings of the egoic mind, or that puts you in touch with the profound stillness within. A teacher may come along who opens your mind and heart, who helps you penetrate your own consciousness in a way you haven't managed on your own, with the result that you learn a great deal about how you keep yourself in thrall to the ego.

All of these things can be a valuable support to your own patient, devoted alertness to your interior, as you move through experience with an eye to learn about yourself, to come closer to knowing what you essentially are.

Having a Spiritual Teacher

There are people in this world who've come to live in the ease and peacefulness of their essential nature. They see clearly, without interruption, the truth that their familiar selves are only incidentally what they are. All of their life experience is carried along in an ongoing knowledge that they are awareness-aware-of-itself. Their lives are not run by unconscious patterns, driven by resistance and attachment. Not subject to mind-generated suffering, they live attuned to the present moment. These individuals are free.

Spending time with an awake person can be transformative. Such a person is living evidence that liberation is a real thing—that the embodiment of the highest human potential is in fact attainable. In the presence of awakeness, it's possible to directly observe the truth that a human life need not be mired in struggle and anguish, at the mercy of every challenging episode. Encountering this state, even as writing or in some other indirect form, can have a deeply transformative impact on one seeking to know the truth.

The presence of awakeness, in whatever form, is an "environment" that enables a recognition of the same higher awareness within yourself. This knowing "recognizes itself" wherever it appears, so that one person's higher self may be enlivened in the presence of another's. Awakeness may be experienced on the level of feeling (in the heart), or it may stir the mind—not the egoic thinker, but the cleanly looking intelligence that's able to simply, freely *see*.

In the presence of awakeness, the natural tendency of the ego-mind to try to understand, to grasp, to reconcile, may be stirred to life. It's important to realize that what the higher state "communicates" cannot be reduced to something the ordinary mind can seize and make sense of. Allow the mind to rest. The other "knower"—the one that's able to directly experience the truth—doesn't need to work at understanding in the familiar way. It recognizes truth, feeling no compulsion to handle it intellectually.

The company of an awakened intelligence can shake things up. It has the power to pull out the props from beneath your accustomed ways of looking at yourself, of defining your idea of "problem," of possibility. It can reconfigure your sense of what's necessary. The profound trust and comfort that occasionally flower in a relationship with a teacher can set in motion real change. A person who lives in the awake state, who's been free of mind and ego long enough to understand how to be of help to another, is able to show you how you collude in your own suffering—if, that is, you're ready and willing to see into yourself without resistance. Such a teacher can give you ways to explore your own consciousness, to be more truly in the present moment, to observe how the ego-mind functions to keep you in illusion about your nature.

The presence of one who deeply knows can function like a mirror, to show you yourself more truly than you've seen before. You may have the sense that the teacher knows you better than you know yourself.

To be deeply *seen*, to be loved unconditionally (perhaps for the first time in your life), is something not readily turned away from. At the same time, it's good to remember that this love is not of the nature of personal, egoic love, and must not be confused with it. Even if it comes in the form of a particular (perhaps beloved) human being, awakeness is in no way personal. It may assume the form of love and tenderness. It may be fierce.

Sometimes those around a newly awakened person, aware of the transformation, will seek the company of this person, hoping that one who's "crossed over" can show the way for others. It's natural to want this, to suppose that one who's "there" might be helpful to those seeking. Yet awakening does not automatically equip an individual to point the way for another. Being a good teacher requires not just awakeness but also discernment, drawing from the insight that grows over time, the sustained reflection that a stable awakening enables. Being an effective teacher involves a measure of skill, as with a teacher in any arena.

A teacher who *knows about* awakened consciousness isn't the same as one who's established in it. There are doubtless wise and capable teachers who aren't themselves awake. Even so, the highest form of teaching can come only from awakeness itself, which perceives the self-limited world of the ego-mind in a way that someone striving to be free of it cannot. If you want to reduce suffering, you may find valuable guidance from a fellow seeker who's a qualified teacher. But if what you want is the radical shift in perspective, it's doubtful you'll receive the necessary system shock from someone who's still seeking to awaken.

Is a Teacher Necessary?

While a teacher can be a valuable support to a seeker, it isn't essential to have one. Many awake individuals never had a teacher. There are people who've awakened (some famously) who never had any spiritual framework, their own misery having been all the "teacher" they needed to push them out of their heads and into reality.

Maybe you've had a teacher, or several. Perhaps you have one now, or wish you did. A given teacher may take you so far, and then another one may push you beyond where you could go before.

Don't go looking for a teacher. If a gifted one comes your way, count your blessings, but don't expect the experience always to be comfortable. If what you're looking for is to feel better, by all means do not put yourself in the hands of a real master.

Don't become fixated on this. Don't think you're doomed to a life of unconsciousness if you can't find the right teacher.

There is, in the end, no illuminator like life.

The *inner* teacher of open-eyed inquiry is the one indispensable element of transformation. There's no change agent like ongoing self-awareness as you move through experience. No one can teach you as much as your own unresisting attention to yourself, in the moment.

If you have a teacher or a spiritual practice, don't assume you always will. Spiritual supports can be helpful—until they no longer are. It may not be easy to come to terms with realizing that a practice, or the presence of a beloved teacher, no longer serves you. Don't let that reluctance lead you to linger there just because it's comfortable.

5

What Is It to Become Free?

When you wake up, when you become established in the knowledge of what you deeply are, you've become free of illusion, the primary one being that you *are* what your mind says you are. You are free of seeking, since you've found yourself to be (already) where you've always wanted to be.

Living as a free being, you no longer experience yourself as the center of the universe. The important thing about whatever life holds isn't how it affects you, what you think or feel about it. The important thing is the plain fact of it. You are free of whatever has been challenging or unresolved. Nor is there the familiar vivid impression of your being a particular individual, in any significant sense, or of being separate or fundamentally different from other people—or from anything at all. Because your sense of identity has changed, your feelings can no longer be hurt, nor can you take offense. You're no longer subject to others' opinions of you (favorable or unfavorable). When you become free of the illusion that you are your ego-mind, there's no longer someone to maintain, protect, or enhance.

Even when something happens that affects your life directly, you don't experience it as having an impact on your deep nature. If you learn you have terminal cancer (which clearly has everything to do with your physical well-being), you don't slip into the belief that a tumor-riddled body is what you *are*.

You've become free of fear. If you're confronted with something that requires action, you're able to move forward with that. If there's nothing to be done, you simply relax into what-is—even if it's difficult. As regards possible future challenges, since they are not presently real, you do not fear them.

When you live in freedom, your inner state is no longer determined by the situation you're in. You experience a steady sense of the real—the sensation of *beingness*—that isn't subject to fluctuation.

Even as your identity is no longer determined by what happens in life, or by what your mind tells you is true, you're thoroughly attuned to what-is. There's no impulse to resist anything, nor is there any need to assess what something means, to assume a response is necessary. Whatever is simply *is;* that's your primary orientation to life. No longer at the mercy of judgment and reactivity, you've ceased to live as though your beliefs are reality. The familiar felt need to have an opinion about anything is gone.

Because an awake person experiences the newness of each moment, unencumbered by whatever has come before, there's an almost childlike delight in living, a perennial freshness of encounter, with even familiar things and people and experiences. The capacity for fun, for spontaneity, for carefree engagement with whatever life delivers is boundless. Beliefs, memories, conditioning, and language do not put themselves between awareness and whatever it's attending, which means there's no intervening "filter" to color the experience of the moment. The encounter is direct, unmediated by anything in the mind. The names for things and categories they're ordinarily placed in (including good and bad) do not automatically spring to awareness, nor do inner commentaries typically accompany experience. A thing is just itself. You've become free of expectation, so that when something out of the ordinary takes place, something sudden or even unprecedented, you take it in stride. This is because you don't go around carrying a background expectation that things will be a certain way (including the way they've always, somewhat predictably, been before).

There's an ongoing sense that things *just happen*. Gone is the familiar impression of there being a you (or a someone else) that's doing something. In part, this is because your sense of where "you" leave off and the rest of the world begins doesn't feel significant. Moreover, you don't experience yourself as separate from the living moment. What you do and what you are, in a given *now*, are a unity. In the experience of both time (doing) and space (location), the accustomed boundaries are not a part of perception. Ease attends all you do; this is part of the sense that everything just happens. Things seem to unfold without strain. There's a freedom from effort, even as you're able to apply yourself with focus and perhaps great force, if the situation calls for it.

In freedom, you do not seek security, because you don't live in the future, and you don't experience yourself as being at risk. "You" are all-that-is, and it's understood that within all that is, things simply are as they are. You're blessedly free of any discomfort with not knowing, with not being able to control, predict, or understand a thing. You're at ease in the presence of instability.

When you are free, you no longer experience attachment—to the roles you play, to possessions, to ideas, to the outcome of action, to the people you love. You are free of ferocious desire, of the driving "need" to get (and keep) what you want. Even so, you have a rich capacity to savor, to experience pleasure. You can still love, still enjoy, still (yes) *want*—prefer one thing over another—but getting it or not getting it will feel very much the same to you, since (as always) whatever *is* is always primary, obliterating in a subtle (but potent) gesture of "is-ness" anything that *might* have been.

Love in the awake state is unencumbered by attachment and the fear it engenders. In normal life, where the ego holds sway, love often is tied up with need, with desire and the longing for fulfillment. In awakeness, where there's no need for ego gratification, love is free to flow without fear of loss, without grasping or the wish to change the other person. Without need or fear in the picture, you're able to love unconditionally. You don't need to be loved; you don't need to be needed. But when love is in the picture, it's wide-open, generous, without constraint.

Liberation means you are free of identification with all that has defined you in the past: your beliefs, roles, history. Some of these things will still function, in a superficial or practical way, but you no longer take your sense of self from them.

You've become free of the tyranny of the mind. It no longer runs you; rather, it serves at your pleasure. Its default condition is quiet. If you need to think about something (usually something practical), your mind is able to function with remarkable clarity, creativity, and efficiency. When you're finished needing to think, you are able to stop, leaving the mind to rest. You've become free of mind-caused stress, of anxiety.

The underlying "feeling" state is stillness, alertness, a subtle orientation of tenderness. If you're in the presence of suffering, you may feel it, perhaps even keenly. (You can also readily decline to "go there," if you choose, simply by directing your attention elsewhere, or by declining to put it anywhere at all.) If something difficult comes to your own life—the loss of someone you love, or physical discomfort—you surrender fully to the pain. You're not afraid of feeling the fullness of whatever is real here and now. You've become free of the habit of resistance.

Being free means freedom from time. You're free of the belief that something important can happen *in* time. Of the sense that the future has the potential to make things better, or that there's something to be feared in the possibility of change or loss. You're free of ambition, of the idea that you need time in order to finally experience fulfillment, and free too of the constant feeling that you don't have enough time. You are free of hope, and free of the burden of the past, of all it has delivered you: the weight of memory, of conditioning, of patterns, of unresolved anguish. *New* life—unfolding life, as it comes moment to moment—is not felt to cling to you anymore, to be carried over (as residue in the form of emotion or thought) into whatever is next. As each moment happens, it is felt quickly to be gone, supplanted by the compelling reality of *this* moment, and now again *this* one. New conditioning does not take place.

Living in the present means you don't particularly look forward to things (as before, when looking-forward-to was a way to endure the imperfect present). This is not because you believe nothing fun or rewarding is in the future. It's because the future doesn't feel real.

Nothing is real but now. And now is enough. It's abundant.

What It's Like—And What It's **Not** Like: Misconceptions About Being Awake

There are common misconceptions about what it is to be awake—what life lived in that "state" is actually like. When people say they want to wake up, their longing is sometimes based on erroneous assumptions about what it would be like for them.

Life doesn't stop being itself when awakening takes place. What is utterly changed is how you experience it, and yourself in it.

One of the primary (and dramatically changed) features of an awake life is its complete ease in the presence of reality. It's this, above all, that accounts for the equanimity that's one of the hallmarks of the liberated state. Sometimes it's supposed that the causeless joy and peacefulness associated with awakeness come somehow *in spite of* reality—that the ongoing ease of the state is due to being at a remove from ordinary life.

This misunderstanding is natural when you consider that many people's reason for wanting to awaken is that they find reality difficult. They want relief from their very lives. There's an assumption that equanimity is inconsistent with an awareness of suffering (violence, poverty, injustice). When someone is known to live in awakeness, it seems that person must be at a distance, in some way, from the real world. The assumption underlying these misunderstandings is that a person's inner state is determined by the outer situation. (That belief is at the heart of unconsciousness, and has everything to do with why the self-made prison endures.)

The desire to experience heightened mystical states (or to get them to last) is sometimes a motivating factor in a person's longing to awaken. But an awake person doesn't live in a state of constant bliss. While leaving behind the narrow definition of self-as-ego does open a person to the encounter with all-that-is, mystical states in no way typify moment-to-moment awakeness. The default condition is more of a quiet neutrality, a presence without obvious feature, perhaps tending toward a subtle delight—a constantly renewed delight at mere being.

It's sometimes supposed that when you're awake, you don't experience pain of any kind. But this is not so. You've ceased to create *mental* (or emotional) causes of suffering. It's true that the ongoing sensation of *being*-aware-of-itself is vaguely pleasurable, palpable, a thing (almost) with fragrance. And the presence of an alive attentiveness is felt around the edges of even a difficult life experience. But the fullness of life sometimes delivers painful things. Because there's no inclination to deny reality, and you yield readily to whatever is, occasionally this means feeling deeply some loss. You do not resist grief or physical pain. When someone dear to you dies, or when you learn you've got a serious illness, you give yourself over to sorrow as if you're being folded into the arms of the beloved. The beloved isn't only about happiness or joy; it's about the restfulness that comes with full surrender.

As something painful is experienced, there are two notable differences from the way it was before awakening. In the freedom of the awake state, what's primary is the *fact* of a thing. There's no impulse to resist even something exquisitely painful. In addition, because acceptance is complete, there's no mind-created suffering overlaid on the already keen pain of being with the thing itself. There's no mental commentary, no wish to escape, no consoling conceptual framework, no useless going over what-might-have-been. The encounter with what-is happens on the level of pure feeling. There's nothing mental in the picture (except for the practical need for thinking that the situation might summon). Full acceptance means there's no subsequent residue from the experience. So the natural "suffering" that comes of a difficult life event is not compounded—or needlessly extended—by anything the mind might bring to the situation.

My friend Anne Chandler has clearly described the feeling state of awakeness, in the fullness of its experience of life: "Going through life without a buffer to dull the joy and ecstasy also means going through life without a buffer to dull the pain and sorrow." As the sage Skin Horse explains to the Velveteen Rabbit, "When you are Real, you don't mind being hurt."

An awake person is not motivated by virtuous ideals. Awakeness makes no effort to be kind or loving, to care for everyone uniformly. Yet compassion is naturally in the picture. It isn't that the impulse to be compassionate has triumphed over self-interest, or that an awake person is somehow *managing* base impulses or the tendency to be judgmental. Liberation makes second nature the concern for others. Unconditional love, patience, tolerance—these are inevitable where there is no judgment, where all of life is experienced as "part of" oneself, where everyone is seen as pure being (and only incidentally the apparent self, with all the attending torment and strain). Awakening is the end of the effort to be compassionate, to behave well, to rein in anger, impatience, frustration. Where there is not the ongoing war with what-is, where acceptance is the norm, there is little possibility for conflict, either within or with others.

An awake person still has a personality, much as before awakening took place, and still has preferences, as well as particular strengths and weaknesses having to do with aptitude and knowledge. The "person" is still here; it's just that it isn't *identified with* as being "who you are." There is still the familiar self—someone who's behaviorally different from other someones, with a particular history, who assumes certain roles, and behaves and speaks in a recognizable way. But because you don't identify with any of it, it's all lightly held. You don't get lost in it. The familiar self never assumes the more compelling reality, as life is experienced. Nor do you experience other people as being primarily their egoic selves (however much *they* still may).

Fleeting Awakenings

It's not unusual for a person to have a short-term awakening, or even periodic awakenings, in which the deep nature is directly known. Someone might have a sustained experience of awakeness and jump to conclude, *This is it, I'm awake.* Yet the awakeness "does not last."

One person's response to this "falling back asleep" will be bewildered despair, while another's will be gratitude—that the pure knowing came *at all* (never mind whether it came to stay). Some will try very hard to replicate what appear to be the circumstances that brought about the heightened awareness. This impulse to attempt to re-create is folly, if understandable, since it's the familiar self that's making the attempt at grasping, trying to re-create, understand, and so on. From within the liberated self, it's understood that the "state" doesn't *go away*—that the perceived need to *hold on to it* or *get back to it* is pure illusion. An illusion that is compelling, to be sure, but an illusion just the same.

Sometimes a person who knows nothing about spiritual enlightenment, or who knows of it but has made no particular effort to awaken, will experience a moment of extraordinary knowing, of seeing the world (and self) with conspicuously different eyes. Reflecting on the nature of the experience, the person will describe the awareness as vividly still and peaceful, suffused with a knowing that all is profoundly well. It's not unusual for a young child or an adolescent to experience this radical well-being, and to recollect it even into old age. However brief, such an experience is stunningly out of the ordinary, in its freedom from distress and its quality of unusual clarity, and is likely never to be forgotten.

It's not surprising that awakeness would sometimes make itself known, only to be swiftly eclipsed by the familiar self reasserting itself, the return to the usual reality. A human being has the ongoing capacity to know higher awareness, the self that's without condition or limitation. Both selves are innate; it's just that usually we're restricted to awareness of the egoic one.

Occasionally, someone will have a sustained experience (even a lengthy one of weeks or months) of awakeness. What's the difference between a fleeting experience and "the real thing"? When the egoic self insinuates its way back into the driver's seat, what happened?

It has to do with the extent to which the familiar self has the more compelling sense of the real. When someone has a significant experience of awakening, during that interval, the primary sense of reality is pure being itself (rather than the egoic self, or whatever is taking place in life). When that person "falls back asleep," what has happened (for reasons that, alas, may not be discoverable) is that the impression of what's real has reverted to the familiar one. The accustomed "content" of reality (what the person is used to experiencing as substantial and important) has reasserted itself. Once again, the conditioned self, the contents of the mind, outer events, the sensation of time—it has all assumed the appearance of reality, and in the process, the felt presence of the "other" that recently was so real has faded.

The question is, which is a person's *default* sense of the real? At some point, when an awakening is stable, the higher self has assumed the default status of the prevailing reality.

The familiar self has such enduring substance and powerful momentum, with the desire to keep itself going, that it can reassert itself many times, over a long period, before it (in effect) ceases to believe in itself.

When the "big" awakening finally comes, the perspective shift it entails is so dramatic and thorough that the sense of the real has been fundamentally altered. The ego- and mind-saturated self is no longer able to convince you of its reality.

Why Awakening Happens

When someone awakens—not fleetingly, but once and for all—is it possible to say why it has happened? Why now but not before; why this person and not another? It's the sort of thing about which there is much wondering, fueled by the longing to leave behind the life of suffering. You might naturally think that if you could know what seemed to precipitate another's awakening, that information might head you in the right direction.

If you ask an awakened person what tipped him over, or (if it were not so gentle) throttled him out of illusion, he may say he has no idea. If you ask another, she may give you a theory. Whatever the offered explanation, it will only ever be a theory. Even if one of them could tell you with some kind of confidence what caused the final letting go of the narrow sense of self—even if such a thing were knowable—it wouldn't be of help to anyone else.

Anyhow, all that can really be said is what was going on right before the shift happened (if indeed the actual moment was observed). But there's nothing to say the relationship was causal. The just-before thing may have had nothing whatever to do with the awakening. Maybe it was just the environment in which the shift occurred (but it could just as well have been some other).

A thousand unnoticed things move a person toward finally putting the burden down, most of them never consciously intended, or remembered in the aftermath. Who is ever to say what the last gesture was? When a person is ready to break loose, nothing will be able to stop it. Something will happen, and if not one thing, some other.

Just try to get in the way of somebody who's really and truly ready to be done with illusion. (Not to say such a person is consciously aware of this heightened readiness.)

You simply don't know why it happens when it does, and even if you knew, knowing would be useless. We are not in charge of how it happens, or whether. So if it happens to someone you know, just be glad of it, and let that be enough. Resist the temptation to draw conclusions about your own process.

Yes, it can reasonably be conjectured that leading up to the radical perspective shift, there must have been a gradual undoing (or a dramatic all-at-once undermining) of the familiar sense of self: a removal of moorings, a growing disinclination to take self seriously, to cling to defining identities or beliefs. Something like that may have happened.

Some awake people seem always to have been joyful, prone to gladness, to gratitude, with a generosity of spirit that's authentic (rather than contrived, overlaid on top of negativity). There's been a constitutional predisposition to lightheartedness.

But then there are the many accounts of someone in the black hole of despair, wanting to die, no incentive to continue.

All illusion of the substance and value of the egoic self had been fried by life, all the circuits blown, the familiar self no longer able to hold up, or no longer bearable. Nothing to embrace, nothing to stand on, care about, reach for. Then—*wham*: the great breaking-open, the collapse, the flooding in of light. Straight from devastation into a stunning delight. All because (apparently) such a one was no longer able to experience personhood as being worth anything.

As for those predisposed to playfulness, gratitude, big-heartedness? Maybe they never took themselves seriously to start with. Or maybe it's that their attention never was all that much on their mind-invented realities, the world around them so enthralling, so undeniably miraculous. Another possibility is this: someone who's joyful, whose constitution is gladness, may be that way *because* of being close to awakening.

It cannot be said that liberation comes more to people with a spiritual practice or a teacher. People awaken who have not gone through any deliberate process of seeking, any effort to become more conscious or to suffer less, and who (moreover) have no idea what's happened to them. Sometimes a person will become free who's never even heard of spiritual enlightenment, having no context for understanding what the dramatic change is about.

There are even people (the highest of ironies) who *were* seeking awakening but who—when it actually happens—fail to recognize the thing for what it is. It doesn't match their prior ideas, which says a lot about the limited ability of the mind to imagine the condition. The higher consciousness cannot hope to be understood by the lower. Erroneous ideas about awakeness, developed previously, can mean it's hard to recognize.

All the conjecture in the world is just gymnastics for the mind, which is a good part of the problem in the first place. There is simply no uniform picture of the person who comes to full awakening, no way to say why it comes when it does.

Your business is not to conjecture, to look for patterns or reasons. The business of one who longs to know the truth is simply to prepare the way, so that if it wants to come, there will be a room full of open windows and doors for it to enter through.

Slip the pins from the hinges; jimmy all the locks. Get out of the way. You cannot mastermind the game, but for God's sake, you can decline to score points for the other side. Omit no opportunity to aim the flashlight of awareness on your own interior, so that you might learn how you keep the familiar self going.

That is your business, to look. Look and look. Do not avert your eyes. Do not wince at what you see. Don't pronounce yourself wicked, or hopeless, or dumb. Open your eyes and see the made-up thing you are. Just that. It may become funny. Avoid getting glum. That's the last thing you should do. Keep looking until it becomes ridiculous, until you split your sides laughing at how seriously you used to take yourself.

Why Is It So Rare?

Clearly, awakening has to do with more than mere wanting, or else lots of people would be awake.

If innate to us all is this condition of unwoundable well-being, why is it so rarely assumed as the primary state? Why is a human life so seldom lived *as that?*

The rareness of the phenomenon might be pointed to as "proof" that the condition isn't in fact innate to everyone. Maybe as an indication that the liberated state isn't even a real thing. When somebody seems at peace through any situation, however challenging or painful, something else (the argument goes) must account for it. Denial, aloofness, a loose screw. Then there's the idea that a few remarkable individuals have somehow earned this condition, been anointed, as it were, or have accumulated sufficient merit over lifetimes.

But no.

All of that ends up getting used as a way to be lazy, or to dismiss the whole thing, either to pronounce it nonsense, or (if you believe it's real but not within *your* reach) to declare yourself not among the chosen few, with no hope for attaining freedom. Those ideas can provide a way to turn from the wanting, from trying to discover the liberated state within yourself—thereby fulfilling the prophecy that it will never be realized, because you do nothing to assist.

Why is it so rare?

For the great part of humanity, awakening isn't even on their radar because they can't imagine any big-picture alternative to the way life is. They don't look outside the closed container of their self-referential lives to wonder about the nature of reality. Plenty of people are *okay* with the way it is. Life is good enough, enough of the time, that they're fine with it continuing the way it has always been. And if you press those for whom life is *not* so good—those who are deeply depressed, or living in situations delivering a steady diet of suffering—they will say, almost to a person, that the only way to make things better is to improve (or escape) their condition. That is, to fix the familiar self or its circumstances. They never question the belief that the life of the conditioned self is adequate as a source of delight, security, and meaning. They think the only hope is to address the depression; to improve the health, financial situation, relationship; to engage in more enjoyable and satisfying activities.

Rarely does anyone look at the whole setup of what is supposed to make life okay, and question *that*. Step outside of the whole thing and ask: *Is all of that what I'm deeply about? Is there more to me than what can be affected by all of the circumstantial stuff?*

For the tiny part of humanity that *does* ask the elemental question about self and reality (some of whom are brought to do so by despair over the ordinary approach to life), even among those, awakening seldom occurs. Why is that? Why—even when a person sees it's possible, and even when abundant attention is devoted to awakening—does it still so rarely come about?

It's because even those individuals almost always go about it incorrectly. They think the task is to change themselves (about which more will be said). And very likely, they have not yet seen (probably are not willing to see) the depth of their attachment to ideas of who they are, and the extent to which they hold on to beliefs because of thinking their thoughts are "true." They simply have not gone deep enough, far enough, into what they identify with. They have no idea to what extent they collude in their own imprisonment.

Also, when it comes right down to it, most who say they want to become free of it all don't *really* want that. They want to keep believing in the substance and value of their conditioned selves. It's just that they also want to *feel* better, to hurt less, or maybe to have more blissful or mystical experiences. They want to get rid of what's painful but keep the good stuff going. Above all else, they want to hold on to the familiar sense of who they are. Maintain the comforting things, the satisfied desires, the illusion of security. But do not—above all do not—come near to anything that feels like a death.

6

Getting Real

Given that the longed-for state of freedom is about living in harmony with reality, even as you never lose touch with the higher knowing, it stands to reason that "getting there" would involve a willingness to be *real*. Real, above all, with yourself.

The end and the means are the same. This is one of the great lessons of the spiritual life. Moving toward awakening asks you to *be* awake, in this moment: to be present with whatever the truth is. To *see* in an unflinching way what is before you—not only what's happening around you, but even more crucially, what's happening within. To feel what's alive in you—however unpleasant, however "unspiritual," it may be.

If you want to wake up, the place to start—right now, regardless of what's occurred prior to now—is to take a real look at where you are and what you want for yourself.

Being truthful with yourself is more important than even the most ferocious wanting. It will get you further than a head full of learning or good intentions. It will certainly carry you well beyond where you'll go if you stay stalled in avoidance, and driven by ideas that are out of alignment with the truth, at a remove from the reality of what's going on for you.

What Do You Want?

You may have been at this seeking for years. Perhaps you've immersed yourself in multiple practices and traditions, sat at the feet of a variety of teachers, spent thousands of hours on cushions, stayed in monasteries abroad, read more books than you can name. Assessed how you were doing at various points, felt some real change take place, watched yourself seem to backslide. Observed others at the same thing, one or more of whom might appear to have eventually awakened. Tried to avoid feeling envy, or plain bewilderment at your own inability to get beyond where you are. You may have given up more than once, but later felt yourself trying again, taking a fresh start.

Maybe you've taken it for granted, perhaps for a long time, that your deepest longing is to wake up. Almost as if it doesn't even bear asking the question.

Or maybe this whole thing is new to you.

It doesn't matter how much you "know" or how much you feel you have to learn. Wherever you are, whatever's happened so far in your life as a seeker, ask, now: *What do I want?*

Not that wanting is automatically getting. But if you hope to get anywhere, knowing what you (really) want is the place to start. If you spend your whole life telling yourself you want one thing when what you actually wish for is something else, you're living in an unidentified misalignment that will keep you stalled forever. You're not aligned with reality—which is the very condition of the longed-for state.

The end and the means are the same. Forget other things, but never forget that.

The answer to the question may have changed over time. It may change again. It's worth asking every so often. Not so much because you'll necessarily get a definitive answer. It isn't even that the answer itself is the big thing. It's the willingness to put the question to yourself that can open a door.

Is your desire really to awaken to your true nature? Or would you just like to feel better?

Take Your Time with This

Before you jump to protest—"Aren't they the same thing? Isn't waking up the ultimate route to feeling good?"—or before you get busy assuming it's somehow second rate to *only* want to feel better, pause a minute. Set aside whatever assumptions might be swirling over the question of what you want. The thing is to look, just look, at what motivates you in your life as a seeker. This is about being real, not about holding on to what doesn't serve you.

Whether what motivates you is the desire to know your true nature, or the modest wish to simply hurt less, to enjoy life more—whatever it is, you're better off being truthful about it. Being real will relieve you of some inner conflict—between what you believe you want and what you're actually doing, between what you "should" work toward and what you *actually* want. The relief of acknowledging the truth will enable you to see more clearly, and it will equip you—*as nothing else can*—to make actual progress.

Looking into the question of where you want to be is related to seeing where you *are*. The invitation is to take a clear-eyed look, which involves courage and (above all) a willingness to forgo self-judgment.

There's no right answer to these questions: *Where am I? Where do I want to be?* Whether you want to be done with belief in your familiar self or just have a more content life, your ability to proceed with openness begins with the letting go of all preconceived notions, including what you've always supposed to be true of yourself.

Where Are You?

You may think you're close to waking up. This could be true. It could also be true that you're a million miles away—that there's so much between you and "it" that you have no idea at all what's in the way of realization.

You may think you're a million miles away, yet you're actually very close.

You may suppose you've come a long way. Or that because you have powerful meditation experiences, you must be close to dropping all illusion.

Whatever you think, chances are pretty good your own assessment is off the mark. The mind is constitutionally limited in its ability to know much of anything in this business. Over-reliance on the thinker (which thinks it can know things like *where you are*) is part of what awakening dissolves.

Still, it's helpful to put the questions to yourself. If only so you don't get settled in an assumption that's subject to change.

If you go around committed to the idea that you want to be done with illusion, ask yourself this: *If I want so much to wake up, why hasn't it happened? What's in the way?* Not that you might come up with the right answer. Still, the willingness to second-guess yourself can till the soil for continuing insight.

If you're ready to wake up, it will happen. Nothing will be able to prevent it. If you're not, more needs to happen.

Are you stuck? Have you been in the same place for a long time (maybe comfortably so), perhaps telling yourself you've gotten as far as you can? Maybe you're maddened by being stuck because you have no idea what the problem is, or how to keep moving. Simply being willing to acknowledge that you're in a stall can help get you moving again. It nudges you to get a little more real—to see deeper into yourself.

You can be only where you are. Seeing that is the beginning of moving on.

Is Waking Up What You Truly Want?

Are you willing to stop identifying with the person you've been for decades? Or do you want to keep yourself intact, hoping to wake up anyhow?

Do you want liberation above all other things? *Instead of* all other things? Are you willing to do whatever it takes?

Do you want this the way a drowning person wants a drink of air?

Is your hunger to know the truth the primary driving force in your life? Or do you enjoy the highs and lows, the energy of striving, the excitement of desire and acquisition?

Do you see loss and suffering as the price that must be paid for the heights of joy?

Do you see the prospect of awakening as the fix for your problems? If your biggest problem were solved, would you still want to wake up?

How do you believe awakening would change your life? Do you imagine you'd be constantly blissful? At a remove from reality?

Do you experience "regular" life as being in conflict with spirituality? Do you use spiritual ideas or practices to avoid challenges in your life? Do you identify with your spiritual practice, attainment, beliefs? Do you cultivate spiritual behavior? Do you avoid difficult feelings? Are you intent on self-improvement? How seriously do you take yourself—your egoic self?

Many people who say they want to awaken lose track of the longing when things are going well in their lives. Then, when something challenging comes along, the interest in the spiritual life will be renewed. Wanting to get off the roller coaster isn't the same thing as wanting to continue the ride but hoping the high points outnumber the lows. The interest in ending the ride altogether is likely to grow during the down times, but then something good happens, and life doesn't seem so bad after all (though that concession probably isn't made consciously).

There's nothing wrong with wanting to minimize the rough spots in life. Just don't confuse that with wanting to be done with the whole thing.

What is your orientation to reality, as you actually experience life? Would you rather distance yourself from reality or yield to it? Awakeness is at home with reality, just as it is, without resistance or the need for interpretation. Most people, including spiritual seekers, would prefer to *escape* reality. Witness the longed-for relief sought in long meditation sessions and retreats away from "regular life," the guilty avoidance of unspiritual thoughts, feelings, and behavior. Not to mention the gravitation toward numbing substances, the computer screen, entertainment that's mindless and heartless.

Living in awakeness isn't about being on a constant high. Being liberated from delusion doesn't deliver you into a state of unending bliss. If anything, it's a neutral state. The relief from mind-caused suffering is initially experienced as pleasurable, to be sure, but only because of the contrast with one's entire preceding life. Once you've assimilated the new way of being, there's a quiet equanimity, with a conspicuous absence of the familiar highs and lows. When you've stopped feeling like the center of the world or the moment, life can be pretty unremarkable.

It's Okay Not to Want to Wake Up

It really is. Waking up is not required to have a perfectly fine life. (It better not be, since it hardly ever happens.) It's entirely possible to be reasonably happy, enough of the time, just by making an effort to be more conscious, less reactive, more present. You can have joy and delight, some fulfillment, a decent set of coping mechanisms (including, maybe, a spiritual practice that gives solace), and relationships that are rewarding enough, without ever waking up, or even trying to.

Declaring that your life is okay as it is doesn't constitute a failure. Perhaps your spiritual work has brought you to where you're not overly resistant, not trapped as you once were in belief that generates suffering. Maybe your daily life is carried along in a pretty steady self-awareness. Do you roll better with life's punches than before? Are you less constantly in your head than you used to be? Maybe it's enough to be as you are now.

Better to be real than to torment yourself with wanting (and failing) to awaken, when that isn't actually what's alive in you, as you experience life. Don't confuse waking up with making welcome improvements in your mental or physical health, your circumstances. All of these are worthwhile. They just aren't necessarily about awakening.

Most efforts to improve life have to do, in one way or another, with enhancing the familiar self. They're focused on healing, on feeling better about yourself, on taking steps toward more security or fulfillment. You focus a good deal of attention on yourself and your situation, whereas liberation involves the end of taking any of that very seriously. When you wake up, you stop believing in the substance of the very self you'd otherwise have been working hard to bolster. It would be absurd to think that one kind of effort would move you closer to the other outcome.

Many spiritual seekers who say their wish is to awaken don't actually want what they believe they do. This becomes clear sometimes at the approach to the brink of what feels like a void, where the obliteration of the egoic self seems imminent. With a shocked recognition of what is being asked, the person will recoil. The scale of the loss—the dissolution of the familiar self—is beyond what was bargained for.

Part of the difficulty, at such a moment of reckoning, is that the mind (ever in cahoots with the egoic self) isn't able to imagine life without the ego at its center. It simply isn't possible to picture yourself no longer being here—not without envisioning physical death. You cannot reasonably expect your ego to go along with its own demise. Yet after it's happened, it's clear that "you" (in some sense of the word) *do* still exist—even as it's unmistakable that you're not who you used to be. It's just that *before*, still completely convinced of the reality of your familiar self, you cannot imagine how (short of dying) "you" could cease to be (let alone how that could be a good thing).

Most people who say they long to awaken are not willing to lose themselves. What they want to lose are their problems, their painful history, their present-life challenges, their guilt. They'd like to hold on to themselves, though—to retain their identity, their sense of accomplishment. They want to continue to enjoy the familiar sources of satisfaction. Most people (even though they may be tired of suffering) actually *like* themselves. They enjoy their "personhood." They revel in their sense of continuity, their developing history, their perceived clarity about who they are, what they stand for. They truly believe they would miss themselves if they weren't there anymore. They want not to lose themselves but to *improve* themselves. Few are willing to go straight toward what feels like a kind of death: the end of all identification with who they think they are.

They say they want to wake up, but their idea of what that means isn't in line with reality.

Ironically, the self that longs to be happy and stress-free doesn't actually experience an improvement upon awakening. *Because the self that seemed to need "fixing" no longer feels real.* For one desiring to know the truth, the focus should be not on trying to help that self feel better, but on understanding the nature of the identity that thinks its improvement will amount to fulfillment. Among the things seen on awakening is the nature of the self that has supposed the "problem" was its inability to provide a satisfying life for itself.

For some individuals, the drama of life's ups and downs is like sustenance. It's how they feel their aliveness. They thrive on it, even if it sometimes hurts. Some of them have undertaken earnest spiritual journeys. Yet if they're honest with themselves, they'll see they aren't willing to say goodbye to the romance of it all. But then it becomes necessary to allow that the down part is the price of getting the good part—to get real that they'll never be able to have the one without the other.

Awakening ends identification, and it undoes the structure that enables desire and its satisfaction. When you consider that liberation undermines much of what's generated meaning (along the way evaporating your sense of even being a somebody), awakening from the so-called dream could be the very *last* thing you'd want.

If what you want is to live a life that's not full of torment, then relax the pursuit of radical awakening and go forward with that worthy desire. The next section of this book addresses the goal of living with greater ease and less anguish. Such a life is attainable, with sufficient devotion to the task. You'll bring more focus to the effort if you stop thinking it's a means to the end of eventual full-blown awakening—and if you aren't telling yourself that attentiveness to your inner life is somehow a waste if you never attain liberation.

The growing interest in spirituality in the contemporary world has made the idea of awakening familiar to more people. In the western culture, where self-esteem is a prized commodity, where "working on yourself" and therapy are valued routes to self-improvement, spiritual liberation is increasingly held up as a goal of the earnest effort to have a better life. As if the end of identification with the egoic self could be the outcome of a self-help project.

Moreover, the fact that it appears more ordinary people are awakening has driven home the impression that liberation *can* be had, that it's a real thing, and is theoretically available to someone willing to work hard enough to get it. The result of these developments is that it's become *popular* to seek awakening. Twenty years ago, it would have been unimaginable for somebody like Eckhart Tolle to team up with Oprah Winfrey for a worldwide program promoting the value and attainability of spiritual liberation.

Still, liberation is a long way from being a widespread phenomenon. And maybe a lot of people who say they want it would benefit from taking a second look at what actually motivates them.

It isn't better to be one place or the other—intent on self-improvement or on self-obliteration. What's better is to be real with yourself. Then you can get on with taking steps toward bringing about the desired thing.

If the nature of your longing is simply to suffer less, relax into that, however much of a step-down it might seem to be to acknowledge that awakening isn't your true priority. *It's where you are.* For now, it's what's real. Almost certainly, if you remain alert and open, things will change.

The Ground of Being

There are people compelled by a desire to know what J. Krishnamurti called "the ground of being." They are driven by the longing to directly encounter the truth, to not skim the surface of things, to not avert their eyes from reality. For some, it's almost a physical need, a bodied devotion to the stripped-down truth, no matter what it turns out to be; for others, it's more of an intellectual inquisitiveness, an urgent curiosity about the nature of being. There's a consuming need to discover—to encounter—one's own essence, unearthed from whatever life experience and egoic concerns have overlaid it. For these people, nothing matters so much as the search for the truth, and they will gladly subjugate all else to that—including concern for the maintenance of their familiar selves.

Are you one of them?

To be delivered to the truth of being, you must be willing to confront every barrier, every pretense—to avert your eyes from nothing, directing them *toward* whatever would obscure the truth.

You must be that drowning person desperate for air.

If it were easy to wake up, if it didn't ask a person to set aside every other consideration, the world would be full of liberated beings.

The compelling desire to get at the truth may have had its birth in a lifelong suspicion, an inner voice that nothing has managed to silence, that there's more to life than what ordinary experience projects as meaningful. A subtle existential malaise underlies much that goes on, a hunch that life is lived on the surface of things—that humanity universally colludes in an unspoken lie, pretending that all we do matters, when in fact we suspect the thinness of our communal inheritance. There is more, there is more, and we have yet to touch it. To *be* it.

For some, this is the deepest desire. In quiet moments, it maddens. That sense that there is more to this world, more to oneself, than is apparent.

Is this you?

The willingness to see where you are—*even at times when the truth is painful*—is an indication that what you seek is not comfort but the truth. Truth is not always comfortable. Often, as regards mental and emotional anguish (the suffering that's self-caused), the truth is anything but welcome. The willing exploration of your conditioning and all you're attached to, the beliefs and roles you've allowed to define you, that you've hidden behind when you felt under siege—these are what you turn *toward*, not away from. All in the name of getting at what-is. The love of reality emboldens you. All impulse to uphold the flimsily built ego-mind collapses under the force of the single-minded search for the ground of all.

Are you ready to abandon the search for security, for respect and admiration, for meaning? Are you willing to exist in uncertainty, in unknowing? What is it you want to awaken to? Do you want to live in the moment-to-moment encounter with reality, without the intervening commentary of the mind, free of the burden of history and identity?

Are you willing to do whatever it takes? If you are, then abandon whatever you've been doing to nurture the self you only superficially are. Discover what it feels like to care for your physical needs and do your work in the world, without defining yourself in terms of these things. Learn how it alters your perspective when mind-made reality is allowed to dissolve, as you cease to confuse thought with reality itself. Rigorously decline to take yourself seriously. When you see that you are fiercely holding on to yourself, see what you're doing. *Stop.* Don't judge yourself. But for goodness sake stop, or give up this awakening thing once and for all. Do not be lazy. Do not be reactive and resistant. Or if you are, you must see that you are. Then move on to the next moment, unencumbered, eyes open.

If you are not consumed with the longing to get at the truth, then give this up. Remember the drowning person. If waking up ceases to feel like that, then rest from the effort.

It's okay to not want to wake up. But if you want it, cease to want anything else.

It's Not Cut-and-Dried

This discussion about what you deeply desire for yourself should be seen as an invitation into a process. None of it is a fixed thing, settled once and for all. As you change, as life keeps occurring, what you want is subject to development. This is an ongoing exploration, a frame of awareness that moves with you as you live, in full recognition of flux and uncertainty.

The moment is a living thing, vivid and brief. How you experience yourself in it (when you're present to it) will also be that living thing. The stitching and unstitching, the ceaseless reconfiguring, is what you *are*. It's what it is to be alive. Be attuned to that living flux, and unresisting of brevity.

What's important is that you never knowingly allow a conflict within yourself—that you rest always in the truth of what's real for you this moment. Keep an eye on any tendency to cling to a guiding principle, just because it seemed to make sense at one time. The less you hold, the more your hands are open to what's here, unexpected, transformative. In every moment is the possibility for a new discovery, a radical undoing.

You may have had an idea of being on a track to awakening, but then one day you're surprised to find yourself oddly content with where you are. No big shift in consciousness has taken place, but you find you're enjoying your ordinary life, awake enough to this moment, and now this one. You realize the driving urgency to go the whole way has settled down. Not that you wouldn't still welcome awakening, if it were to come. But it's ceased to consume you.

Let it be. See that the idea has released its hold on you. See what that feels like—to just *live*.

See too how the idea itself (as a thought) never really got you very far, except maybe to compound the anguish already inherent to any life. Something else to fail at.

Sometimes releasing the fiercely held project of waking up will be the very thing that drops you off the cliff. You never know. (But it doesn't work to let go *so that* you'll awaken.)

Maybe you've been working on yourself for a long time, hoping to suffer a little less. You've had this idea that only people like the Dalai Lama and Eckhart Tolle attain liberation—that it has to be earned, or bestowed. It's seemed the furthest thing from possible that the whole ego-mind structure could shut down, ceasing to believe in itself. That you might no longer have to work to quiet your mind, to unwind resistance. Little have you imagined that you could live in absolute freedom.

But then one day you find yourself thinking—*Hey, why not? Why the heck not?*

It can be wildly liberating to step inside the possibility, try it on, look around at the terrain of possibility. A place you've never let yourself be before. See what it would ask of you to go toward it. See how that feels, even just to consider it.

You're not the same person you were yesterday, and if you're still here tomorrow, you won't be the same then as you are today. Maybe discovering what you want will turn out to be your life's work.

Everything comes down to being present to this moment.

This *is* awakeness. It's also how you *prepare* to awaken. And . . . it's how you live in equanimity, *whether or not you ever wake up.*

The more focused you are on the now, the more content you'll be. The point really *is*, after all, how do you experience *this* moment? When the present ceases to be lived as a means to an end, you'll be less obsessed with waking up.

It also is true that present-moment awareness is the best possible preparation for awakening.

Part Two

Choice Hiding in Plain Sight

If you begin to understand what you are without trying to change it,
then what you are undergoes a transformation.

—J. KRISHNAMURTI

7

Cultivating Self-Awareness

If you'd like to ease your suffering, here is the place to start: locate its point of origin. You cannot hope for a life of greater equanimity if you don't begin there.

Where Does Suffering Come From?

Whatever you do, don't go looking where you've looked previously. (The results so far probably haven't been very encouraging.) The effort to improve things has likely been misdirected. Any improvement has been short-lived or superficial, because the underlying situation has remained unchanged.

It's natural to suppose that if the *cause* of suffering seems to be "out there," in external things, then the *remedy* would also be there. It appears the way to reduce suffering is to focus on improving the circumstances.

But no.

What you're looking at now is how to significantly change the way life feels—regardless of what comes along.

In a way, the entire spiritual life is about this. It's an ongoing, ever-deepening discovery of your role in determining what life feels like. The discovery is by turns heartening and sobering. There's no way around that.

But if you're willing to stay with it, you'll begin to experience life very differently. Because as you close in on the real cause of suffering, you'll discover in the same gesture the source of peace—finding that it too was not where you supposed.

Learning About Attention

How to get from here to there? From how life is now to a more steadily peaceful condition? How to come to a way of being that's engaged in real life but without the underlying mental torment, low-level anxiety, the grasping for control?

It begins with learning how to look. With attention. Feeling what attention is like, and learning how it differs from thinking. Discovering that attention can be summoned, directed this way or that. Cultivating deliberateness about where it's put.

Attention doesn't exist in the past or the future. It comes alive now. The means and the end are the same. The way to experience your innate awakeness is to be present, and you can do it no time but now.

But you *can* do it. Now, you can.

Do it. Come to wakefulness. Pay attention.

Feel what it is to *look:* how you can gather attention and focus it in a place. The immediate scene; these words you're reading; what someone else is doing or saying; your own thoughts; sensation in your body.

See, it's so ordinary, so unexpectedly absent of anything remarkable, that you can fail to notice it.

It's the beginning of a miracle taking place.

Think of all the projects you've ever undertaken to improve things for yourself. The determination to break a bad habit, or cultivate a good one. Intention, commitment, hoping, resolution. Counting on somebody else to do something, or just waiting for things to happen, for change to come as it naturally will. The cure to take hold. The right administration to come into office. All have to do with something extending out past now.

See how we count on the future?

But this—here, now—isn't about anything that will ever come. It's about this moment, not any other. Even so, present-moment awareness has (yes indeed) everything to do with bringing about a better life for yourself.

So bring attention to something now. See what attention feels like, the deliberateness in it. How if all gathered attention is focused on pain in your foot, awareness is only minimally on the color of the walls of the room. If attention is focused on the voice and face of the person who's telling you something, it's *not* focused on the interior of your head, which might otherwise have been planning the thing you'd say in response, when the time comes.

Attention goes one place or another, unceasingly. Only and always in the present. What happens not so consistently is the *awareness* of where the attention is going. It *just* . . . all on its own, a little like an unruly dog . . . *goes* there. Goes where it will.

As if there were no choice in the matter.

The gold is here. When you look to see where attention is, you find there are options (more than you knew) about what to do with it. Where to direct it, and whether to focus it in a single place, or to direct most of it in one direction while keeping steady background attention elsewhere. Or (the norm, the default) to let it wander at will, as if there weren't an intelligence behind it.

If you want to come to the root of suffering, to understand your role in the flowering of equanimity, you could do nothing more potent than to bring a degree of unwavering attention to your interior. Let your inner state be the one place your attention does not veer from, as each moment gives way to the next.

Even as some attention will naturally be on whatever is taking place outside yourself, don't allow outer reality to be so absorbing that it distracts you from the feelings and thoughts stirred up. They are what to pay attention to. If you want to lead a more peaceful life, the primary focus should shift from external events to the inner, as a general practice.

Each time you remember to bring attention to your interior, first you'll notice where your attention has been (for it is always *somewhere*). Then you'll feel some (or all) of it move to look at what's going on inside.

This is the beginning of a discovery with the potential to be a forceful catalyst for change.

Suffering is not caused by what's going on out there. It's caused by what's going on inside you. But it's useless to take somebody else's word for this. You must discover the truth of it yourself, from direct, patient observation.

Attention and Thinking

Putting attention on your mental and emotional state isn't the same as *thinking* about it. Attending is alert presence. It's cleaner and more reliable than thinking, especially as regards anything egoic.

One of the great discoveries in the life of spiritual inquiry is the difference between attention and thought. A simple way to know which is taking place is to make note of the feeling state. Attention and thought feel conspicuously different from one another.

Attention is encounter, without any charge to it. It simply *looks*. There is a feeling of stillness. Attention is peaceful— whether or not what's focused on appears peaceful itself. The gripping concerns of the egoic self subside in the act of paying attention. What's primary in this awareness free of agenda is the thing being encountered, not the one doing the encountering.

This is true even if it's your own interior you're looking at. A neutral observation is under way, without the familiar need to judge or interpret. Attending is simply being-with, acknowledging the presence of something. There's no resistance, no mental activity, no reactivity.

By contrast, when you think about something, especially something with emotional content, the ego is apt to be engaged. Rather than restful stillness, there's a sensation of effort, of motion. Thinking involves processing, applying prior learning, projecting ahead. There's a tendency to label, analyze, imagine, rehash. Egoic mental effort means orienting one way or another to the object of thought, which seems to reflect somehow on the self. So, even though the focus is a particular *objective* thing, the energy of investment is personal. (It's about *you*, ultimately.) Thinking about something is likely to stir anxiety, excitement, obsessiveness, unlike attending, which is more calm.

A person has the capacity for both and (with self-reflection) becomes able to switch from one to the other. If you realize you're caught in egoic thought, you may be able to step away from thinking and ease into more restful attention. Clarity is nurtured by attention, by contrast with what egoic thinking engenders (defensiveness, angst, pointlessly repetitive thoughts). You'll learn more about your role in your own suffering from clear-eyed attention than from egocentric thought, which cannot hope to get out of its own way.

It's possible to be caught in thought, or swirling in emotion, and see (via attention) that you're caught. Attention occurs outside the realm of thought and emotion. Being able to observe yourself at the mercy of internal forces can vividly illuminate the nature of the familiar self. It can also bring blessed relief: you experience a "part" of yourself not prone to suffer, that isn't subject to the present difficulty. Being in attention brings you into the present. It reminds you there's more to you than ego. Egoic thinking keeps you in your head, at a remove from presence.

Self-Judgment

Attention turned within is different from the inner critic. Clear self-awareness has nothing to do with the conscience cultivated in childhood, when parents, teachers, and clerics tried to install their reprimanding voices (or the deity's) inside you. Attentive observation isn't about guilt, about judgment or assessment of any kind. It doesn't even involve naming what's seen. It simply looks.

Here's where the difference between attention and thinking becomes vivid.

Learning how to do this neutral seeing, free of judgment, without any plan to improve, is for most people a novel experience.

See how it does not come naturally, so practiced as we are at self-judgment. But almost anyone can learn how to do it.

We're so used to thinking that if we're to change, it must begin with disapproving of where we are. Something in us thinks—*If I don't judge myself, how will I ever get better?* What's being proposed here is a different approach. You're a self-aware being trying to discover how much say you have in the way life feels.

What's truly transformative is to see yourself clearly, permitting nothing to interfere with the seeing. To learn all you can about your familiar self, as it's showing up in this moment. To the extent that you feel guilty or embarrassed, that you berate yourself, you'll look away from the truth, compromising your ability to learn. You must see whatever is there, so you can discover how your familiar self operates, how it keeps itself going. You need to realize how hard it works to defend itself, in an ongoing (exhausting) way.

It's part of coming to understand how you collude in your own suffering.

Declining to judge yourself isn't about self-love, justification, or self-forgiveness. Attention involves no consoling ideas about how it's all okay. This is a neutral, objective sort of looking, the way a scientist or an explorer approaches a just-discovered thing. It has to do with curiosity, with wanting to understand. It asks an unresisting willingness to see whatever is there.

When you're observing your inner state, if you feel any tendency to self-judgment, it's an indication you've slipped from clear-eyed attention to ego-focused thinking. It's easy for this to happen (almost automatic, from long habit), but as soon as you notice signs of self-chastisement—discomfort, avoidance, thoughts about doing better—simply return to pure attention. The key is to notice: to see the ego wanting to get in on the action. Just step gently to the side. See the ego as a cartoon character that's broken into the room. Let it barrel right out the back door. Return to plain, unencumbered looking at what's going on in your awareness, including the tendency to judge.

Without judgment, you can see. Clear seeing is the beginning of change. The purpose of observing your interior, in present awareness, is to discover how the prison of the egoic self is built and maintained. As you come to understand how you keep the whole thing going, how the machinery of suffering operates, change begins to take place—without your ever having tried to bring it about. Through the open door of awareness enters a quietly occurring miracle.

Changing Without Trying to Change

It is possible to suffer significantly less, to experience life with greater ease and delight than you have your entire life until now.

But change doesn't come about because of *trying* to change.

When awakening happens, the shocked discovery is that the longed-for condition was present the whole time. What has changed isn't the fact of the matter, but *only* the clarity of vision.

A clue can be taken from this awakened realization, as you (not yet awake) engage in the earnest effort to experience life more peacefully. What's important is not to work to improve, but to learn about how you *already* determine the degree to which you suffer. You're discovering a dynamic that's under way. The focus must be on long-standing habits, lifelong ways of orienting to yourself—*rather than on trying to be different from what you are.*

Transformation is set in motion by seeing where you are now. By seeing how you keep it all going. Change happens entirely on its own.

This isn't about self-recrimination. It's about discovering that you're an active (if unwitting) participant in determining how life feels.

As you learn how you have more to say about suffering than you ever realized, you begin to experience that freedom is *already here.* You discover that option is alive in you. It only remains to exercise it consciously, deliberately. All that really changes is that you become aware of what's been happening right along: that choice has been in the picture all your life. Once you've come to that, you'll naturally decline to create suffering for yourself.

Not overnight. This is a gently unfolding miracle. Be patient. All your life, you've been doing it the other way, believing yourself to be at the mercy of life. Don't expect the whole thing to undo itself all at once. And don't suppose seeing the truth will always be comfortable.

As sips of unaccustomed freedom come to you, you'll be grateful for even small changes. You'll see there is no rush.

Keep attention on your inner world, as you respond to what is. Be willing to go deeper than you've gone before. Without trying to be different from what you are.

What to Notice

Nothing you can learn about suffering from a teacher or a book will come near to the value of what you'll learn from observing yourself in the present. Moment-to-moment life is the great teacher. Putting awareness on the moment, with yourself in it, is a gesture of enormous power. See your orientation to what's happening, how it's affecting you inside.

When your inner world becomes an object of attention, you've stepped outside the ego-mind to watch it functioning. Seeing yourself in the scene, you experience that there's a knower beyond the familiar self.

The reality to look at is *only* this moment, the present scene. This is what's real. Not the larger situation of your life nowadays (which is available to awareness only via the mind, putting you in the realm of thinking-about, rather than attending). Look at what's happening now, what you're doing, the immediate environment—anything directly experienced. The effort to reduce suffering depends on the ability to keep primary attention on the *now*, where life is actually lived, not to allow it to spill over to encompass the big picture.

Notice any thoughts. There may be mental commentary about what's going on, some reference to prior history relating to the present situation. Simply witness the activity of your mind. Notice the way the present moment seems to be about you, to ask some degree of mental/emotional engagement. Observe if you feel positive or negative about what's occurring, or if you'd like something to change. If there's a tendency to resistance or judgment, see that. Notice any feelings stirred up, and any tendency to avoidance of feelings. If there are bodily sensations (tension, discomfort, anxiety, quickening heart), see and feel them. It's all part of the reality of the now.

Be aware of opinions and beliefs, as they appear in your mind. See how values you've habitually held will arrive all on their own, fully formed. Notice memories coming to awareness, and thoughts about what's ahead. Be alert to the presence of hopefulness or dread, any motion toward a possible future. Notice the energy of mental obsessiveness, when it comes, how thinking tries to hold on mentally to something that isn't present now.

See what it feels like to simply observe all of this. Don't be afraid to turn toward it all. Whatever is within, however negative or painful, is no enemy. Eventually, you'll come to see it's all invented. For now, it's information of enormous value as you seek to learn about the role you play in determining what life is like. Insight into how the familiar self functions will penetrate further when you've set aside the lifelong habits of self-judgment and avoidance. Prospects for significant change will grow dramatically, well beyond where they were with force of will, guilt-laden self-control, and grim intention running the show.

If you've been on a spiritual journey for some time, you may have become frustrated, or even despairing, by attempts to "work on yourself": to manage your thoughts, push away unpleasant feelings, quiet your mind, overcome obstacles, cultivate "spiritual" behavior and attitudes. This present approach gives relief from all of that—an effort that's exhausting and largely fruitless.

Be alert to the temptation to take refuge in spiritual ideas as a way to "rise above" uncomfortable truths, to avoid seeing the fullness of what happens inside you. In the attempt to cultivate better habits, you may have been carrying an ideal of how you'd like to be—more tolerant or compassionate, perhaps; less attached or ambitious. Making reference to the internalized ideal of the person you aspire to be and contrasting that model with how you are at present can interfere with the ability to see the frank truth of what's real now. Drop the standards you've held up for yourself. They'll only interfere with seeing where you *are* and, because of that, will be (ironically) in the way of your ever actually embodying them. The standards in your head have everything to do with why you're stuck.

Keep your eyes open.

8

Choice

The degree to which a person experiences choice figures significantly in the impression of freedom or its absence. Choice is most generally understood to be at play in the arena of behavior, action, and decision-making—the choice to live here or there, to eat this or that, to pursue this career or that one.

As self-awareness deepens, and assumptions about the absence of option become available to scrutiny, the role of choice in the inner life is revealed to be a major player in determining how life is experienced.

Making Life Decisions

When the occasion comes to make an important decision, it's certain to absorb a lot of attention. Considering a career change, thinking of ending a long-term relationship, contemplating becoming a parent—passages such as these are undertaken with great seriousness and focus . . . and often with an equivalent measure of angst.

A decision having major ramifications is likely to be "overprocessed" (subject to obsessing, uncertainty, second-guessing), since the perceived risk of taking a wrong direction is great. The mind will project ahead, spinning alternate future scenarios, in the hope that examining the range of possible outcomes will retroactively inform the decision. While scanning theoretical futures can yield information with some value, it's a setup for getting mired in mental pictures giving illusory impressions of reality. All the while, there's the queasy underlying awareness that *I don't really know how it will turn out* and *I'm not in complete control here.* Something in you knows, however reluctantly, that even what looks like a good decision now has only so much influence over how things will actually turn out. But at such a moment, with so much riding on the decision, being real with yourself about the limits of your control and your knowledge is no small feat.

Some people facing a big choice will rely primarily on their minds, supposing rational thought to be best equipped to make a good decision, while others are inclined to "go with the gut," trusting deep feeling or intuition to guide them in the right direction. The two—the mind's ideas and the gut's deeper inclination—may become contestants in an internal debate, each seeking primacy over the other, with one part getting the upper hand one moment and the other the next.

Whether you rely more on thinking or on the "heart," trying to sort out something complex can feel like being in an argument with yourself. One point of view marshals its argument, and then comes a countering set of points, like lawyers in a courtroom. Often, one posture appears to make as much sense as the other, depending on the mood of the moment. The process of trying to come to a final determination can be maddening, utterly consuming. With something big, mental and emotional turmoil is practically a given, part of the atmosphere where the weighing and debating are taking place.

But turmoil never helped anybody make a good decision.

The mind and emotions are prone to self-referential, repetitive, fear-driven processing, all of it in the service of the ego, and therefore bound to generate angst. Seduced by the convincing "reality" of its own creations, the thinking mind is able to drift far from truth—from what's actually known.

Especially where the course of action to be taken will have significant ramifications for your life, and possibly for someone else's, you naturally will want to bring to the process your best available resources.

The Ace in the Hole

At such a time, you'd do well to remember there's more to you than your mind and your emotions. As you make the earnest effort to come to a clear determination of how to proceed, realize there's another intelligence available, one that's outside the turmoil.

By stark contrast with thinking, attention is outside the useless wheel-spinning. It's able to look clearly and intelligently at the situation under consideration. Not to process, not to judge and conceptualize, but simply to *look*. The looking occurs not in service to the ego, ever concerned for its own welfare, but in the service of wisdom. Rather than fear-driven uproar, an atmosphere of calm prevails. There's an alertness, a receptivity, a freshness of perspective. Clarity is a natural outcome of observation with the charge taken out of it.

This is an invitation to explore that part of yourself at a critical moment of your life. To cultivate that clear-eyed point of view, at a time when it can really benefit you. Explore what it feels like to adopt that perspective as you consider the situation that asks for a good decision. Learn what it feels like to pay attention, and how that sensation differs from mentally overprocessing a thing, or cooking it in a sour emotional stew.

The act of simply bringing awareness to the present moment—allowing the mind to rest from argument-marshaling and scenario-spinning—enables you to feel your presence, your plain aliveness. This makes available the other "faculty" that you possess, bringing in the conscious awareness that's without agenda, without angst. Having set aside the ceaseless gear-turning of the mind, you tap into an intelligence not compromised by egoic concerns.

Looking from this uncharged perspective means taking in the scene the way a wide-angle camera would. You're getting the lay of the land, without stepping into it and getting caught up in the drama. Rest from the effort of processing, projecting, comparing, and just hold an awareness of the circumstances. Encounter the unmade decision with the stillness of presence, and see what you see.

Life takes place in the present. The looking happens there, in presence; and ultimately, the course of action will be decided there, in *some* present moment. This is true even in the case of a decision that necessarily takes into account a big sweep of life, having long-term ramifications.

Whereas the fear of making a wrong decision may lead the ego-mind to minimize or deny inconvenient details, pure attention (being free of egoic agenda) is unlikely to experience discomfort in the presence of difficult truths. The neutral looking isn't afraid to see whatever is there. Disengaged from the fear-based wish to control, you're more likely to allow a comfortable recognition of what's not knowable, of what may be outside your control.

Resting from the frenzied search for the right course of action, you may find a decision simply comes with ease, unbidden and unambiguous. Short of that, you will almost certainly see things that you hadn't realized before, when trying too hard to forge a solution got in the way of one revealing itself to you.

Whatever decision ultimately emerges, it's likely to be as good a choice as could be. Still, there's no predicting how things will turn out. It's not as though you have some kind of objective knowledge that all will go well, or that later you'll necessarily be able to look back and declare you did the perfect thing. It's just that you're able to make the best possible decision, given what's knowable now.

Having come through this process, you can proceed into the next phase of life, where the ramifications of your decision are to unfold, with a readiness to accept what comes, even if it's surprising or disappointing. You're able to proceed—to live—without the attachment to outcome that would have gripped you had the decision been made via the gear-grinding ego-mind. And as the decision plays itself out, if you're able to bring to emerging developments the same consciousness you applied to the decision itself, you'll be able to accept what's real then, moving on from there with clarity and ease.

Choice in Surprising Places

Action is the *least* significant realm where choice operates. The truly life-changing choices occur inside, silently, often passively, almost always unconsciously, below the level of seeing. What isn't seen cannot be done differently.

Choice lies quietly in many unexpected places. It's like an animal in hibernation. You come near it many times a day, never realizing it's there. Hiding in plain sight, choice lives in dynamics and processes you might never think to notice. If only you realized it was there, your life might dramatically change.

Have no doubt—the change would be for the better.

Many spiritual revelations are of this nature: places there turn out to be options (which is to say, freedom) *where they had not been seen before.* When someone wakes up, it is all clearly seen. It's a true shock to the system, the discovery of all the places freedom has always been—but unrecognized. Understand: It isn't because of awakening that option now exists. It's that what's seen from the awake perspective makes it possible to recognize the freedom that was there *right along.*

The choices are seen to flower everywhere, abundant as air—ubiquitous as suffering was before. You recall vividly how at the time, it felt as though choice had little part to play in the activity of your mind, in how life was experienced. It's the knock upside the head that says *I needn't have suffered*. But you sure as heck couldn't see that at the time.

Then again, maybe you never thought to look.

How often do we say or think, *I can't help it. It's genetics. It's because I'm a Scorpio. It's my karma. My age. My difficult childhood.* On and on. How many ways we come up with to say, *I'm at the mercy of something larger than myself.*

There's more to it than what we ordinarily see.

The purpose of this present looking is to reach down into the dark of the unrecognized and to pull it up into the light.

Here are some generally unrecognized choices:

- React or not (inwardly as well as outwardly)

- Where to focus attention (the situation or your inner state? the present or some past/future item?)

- Feel your feelings or escape into a head full of defensive/resistant thoughts

- See life as a drain on the spiritual or see it as the arena where aliveness is experienced

- Let circumstances determine your inner state, or not

- Resist or accept

- Let a recent experience cling to you, or let it go (be past)

- Believe your thoughts, or not

- Haul around your painful past, or set it down

- Give attention to something (be with it), or think about it (evaluate, obsess)

- Identify with your conditioning and beliefs, or see them as conditioning and beliefs
- Judge your thoughts and behavior, or witness them
- Judge others, or simply see them
- Use your mind appropriately, or let it run you
- Believe in the absolute reality of your familiar self . . . or decline to

That last choice is the big one, the mega-choice. It's the difference between being awake and not being awake. It's the choice to live as though you're pure ego or pure awareness.

The items on the preceding list are explored in detail throughout this book. But they bear looking at *as a group*. The invitation is to begin to notice how you experience the absence of fundamental choice in your own life—to see if you can find where you draw heavy boundary lines for yourself (placing limits on possibility) and assume that those lines are fixed by some immutable law. Discover the limitations you believe to be inherent to the human (or your particular) condition.

It's the assumptions you don't know are operating that imprison you.

Just by setting in motion a gentle background inquiry into your assumptions about choice or its absence, you can open your eyes to things you've never seen before. This can lead to a shifting of the lines around what's possible for you. The discovery of an unexamined assumption opens the door to the possibility that *I could be wrong*.

Maybe you're not as trapped as you think you are.

The Choice Underlying All Others

We are all two selves. There is the self that's able to suffer. Then there's depersonalized awareness. This self has no gender or beliefs, nor is it affected by experience. It's the same in each person (even in "bad" people, though the mind may not welcome this idea).

This self does not mind a single thing. Imagine.

But it's alive. Exquisitely attuned to the real. It doesn't experience itself as separate from anything. It doesn't age. It does not fear death.

This self is spaciousness. When it notices itself, there's an experience of barely discernible sweetness, like watery maple sap right out of the tree. Not the concentrated sweetness of the boiled-down version, like mystical bliss or physical orgasm. It's subtle. This self is so all-pervasive, so yielding and tender, that it's able to contain the misery and variety of the whole world, all the while sensing its own presence everywhere.

The primary unseen choice that is constantly being made is to identify with something that is not *that*.

Seldom does anyone consciously choose to identify with the familiar self. But every single day, every moment of ordinary life, the identification is ongoing. Even just to recognize that it's happening, to see the artificiality of it, can enable the presence of the other to be sensed.

The other self may be sensed in a moment of particular stillness. A moment when you've become lost in the feathers of a bird you're looking at. A moment on the edge of sleep, or one in which you're riveted on a dancer on a stage. Or when you have a paintbrush or a fishing pole in your hand, and all the world grows still, and there are no problems anywhere that you can find.

The awareness could come in a war zone too—in a situation where things are so terrible that you could die the next moment. Yes, it can be in such a place and time that this thing comes to you. People have spoken of knowing this exquisite self when they were in death camps, sensing the living presence of a reality apart from the hideous one they were trapped in.

It is everywhere, always. Like maple sap, thin as water, it runs, spills, soaks all it touches. Including you, at your essence. *This is what you are.* Directly sensing this, you take the rest of what you are to be incidental. It becomes lightly held. Even as people you love die. Even as there are wars. Even as the polar ice caps are melting.

I'm trying to tell you something.

We choose every moment we live to identify with something limited and in constant flux—with our narrowly defined selves. We can opt not to. It may not look as though we have option. That doesn't mean we don't.

We are, mostly, blind.

9

How Life Affects You

What you make of what happens matters more than what happens.

It matters *a lot* more.

In fact, as regards the cause of the common kind of suffering, what you make of a thing is the entire story. Which is to say, outer events and circumstances don't "cause" you to suffer. *You* do that.

For the time being, we are setting aside suffering caused by physical extremity—pain, starvation, imminent danger, and so on. What we are looking at is mental and emotional suffering. That is, invented suffering, *optional suffering*.

The suggestion that *you,* not outer reality, are the cause of your own suffering may be somewhere between bewildering and infuriating. The idea that choice is at play here could be interpreted to mean a person would deliberately inflict pain on self. No one of reasonable mental health, of course, would knowingly do that. The key here, as in so many areas having to do with consciousness, is the discovery that choice exists where it did not appear to be.

Hang in there. You have more latitude than you've realized about the extent to which you suffer. We're talking about the possibility of freedom. Real change in your life. It stands to reason you will be asked to question some deep assumptions.

The Deep Motivator

You want to alleviate the pain. You want to be happy. That is the goal—the deep one—motivating much of what you do. You tell yourself the way to accomplish that is to solve the problems that appear to be causing the torment and dissatisfaction—get a better job, heal the illness, find love. Seldom do you question the underlying assumption that your problems are what cause unhappiness.

The connection between the two must be teased apart, and the attention redirected—away from the focus on changing reality, and onto the underlying motivation. Which isn't to solve problems *per se,* but to be content. Instead of asking *What can I do to fix things?* ask *What do I need to do to stop hurting?* Examine the unquestioned assumption that there's a fixed relationship between your inner state and how things are going in your life.

The problem isn't that things in life are imperfect. The problem is that you believe your difficulties are what you *are*—that it seems well nigh impossible to be okay alongside them. Learning to be okay in the presence of challenges doesn't mean you can't work to improve things. It's just that there's no longer so much riding on their resolution.

You might still want to find love, but you no longer believe you need to have love to be happy. The illness may not find its cure, but you might be able to find equanimity even as you continue being sick.

The Relationship Between Outer and Inner Reality

Something takes place in your life, a thing that draws your attention, and you have some kind of orientation to it. There's a response inside (thoughts, feelings), and maybe an outward one (something done, said). The orientation is likely to have a quality, even if only subtly, of the positive or the negative, sometimes with a mix. Seldom, if a thing has gotten your attention, is its effect on you truly neutral.

The orienting-to-reality is pretty much ongoing, throughout the course of a day, a life. The inner narration is like a real-time soundtrack, seldom interrupted, being produced on the fly. The propensity to ceaselessly evaluate probably was set in motion long ago in the species' evolution, because of the survival-driven need to be constantly alert to the possibility of danger. Attunement to what's happening, with the felt need to respond, is so much a part of humankind that seldom would anyone bother to remark on it. It's assumed that when anything significant comes across your radar, you'll have *some* response to it: a reaction, a comment, an opinion, a feeling.

Any thoughts that come, as well as emotions they give rise to, become identified with the occurrence. They're fastened onto it, as though they were inherent to it. This process is taken for granted, as "natural" a phenomenon as reality itself. By this means, whatever you tell yourself about what's happened becomes reality, for you—a reality that's an expansion of the thing that's happened. The power of the interpretive mind to produce a convincing rendering of a real-life occurrence is such that the resulting story looks like "the truth." The outcome is that you inhabit a mind-made version of reality (that prison), *as though it were objective reality itself.* If any emotion or behavior comes about, in response, it's been set in motion *not* by the occurrence itself, but by what you've told yourself about it.

But (*this is key*) you will naturally tell yourself that your thoughts and emotions were *caused* by the thing itself. You'll believe that option didn't enter the picture until the point at which you chose to speak or act.

This is one of the prime ways the prison cell is constructed, and how we manage not to realize that the prisoner and the builder are the same.

If you believe the outer circumstance is yoked inevitably to your story about it, then you will surely be at the mercy of whatever is going on in your life.

Ordinarily, as we're taught about right action, both in the realm of ordinary socialization and in the world of spirituality, what's emphasized is the role of choice in *behavior.* We're encouraged to look at speech and action as being subject to some degree of choice, which generally means controlling or moderating (or concealing) whatever is alive within. The assumption is that a person has no say in determining the thoughts or emotions behind the behavior.

This present discussion is not about choice in behavior but about what goes on *inside* you—that is, the mental and emotional response that *precedes* any behavioral one. This isn't an invitation to practice self-discipline, to apply force of will, or to engage in concealment. You aren't being urged to "control your behavior" even as your interior is in full flare (though self-control is surely advised, if the behavior would cause harm).

If you aren't having a strong *internal* reaction, you won't *need* to pretend or to manage any outward reaction.

The management of behavior does little to reduce your own suffering. Declining to act on your base impulses (thereby keeping things from getting worse than they already are) is a poor cousin to greater equanimity. The key to reducing suffering is to be found by moving inside—by bringing attention to the thought and emotion that give rise to outward expression.

If you want to suffer less, omit no opportunity to step outside your mind and watch what it's doing with reality. As long as you're trapped in the world constructed of your thoughts-about-something—as though they were actual objective truth—you *will* suffer.

The Appearance of No-Choice

Once a body of thoughts and emotions has flowered in response to something that's happened, and all of it becomes affixed to the outer thing itself, it's inevitable you'll suppose your inner response (and perhaps behavior) couldn't be other than it is. The idea that choice has been operating will simply not compute. Any responsive attention or effort will inevitably be directed toward the outer situation (perceived to be the cause of the trouble), *not* at your interior. In focusing on the outer situation, the operating assumption is that the only way to feel better is to address the (outer) "cause."

Because we want, above everything else, to *feel better*. Always this is the deep motivator. The assumption of a causal relationship between what happens in life and how we are doing inside goes largely unexamined, with the result that we apply our attention almost exclusively to addressing particulars of circumstance and event as the way to improve the way life feels, altogether bypassing the role we ourselves might be playing in generating the misery.

Not that there's anything wrong with addressing a situation that needs attention. It's just that action to improve something should be taken for its own sake (not so you'll feel better), and should not be confused with the question of how it's affecting you.

They are distinct phenomena.

In fact, any effort to improve real-life issues will be more fruitful (and less stress-inducing) if you're simultaneously putting some attention on your interior.

If you want life to be better, there's nothing more potent you could do than to explore the ways you keep the outer and the inner yoked together, as though they were a single thing.

Causality

Picture yourself in a situation with the power to rile you, or to put you in a state of anxiety. It's something that would reliably elicit a strongly negative inner response and possibly a behavioral one, something that's actually happened, or that you can readily imagine. Allow yourself to "go there" (as realistically as you can).

Say you do your self-employed tax return and find you owe a lot of money. This results in distress, as well as self-recrimination for having neglected to make quarterly payments throughout the year. Or you hear your ex is telling stories about how hard you were to get along with, which infuriates you, as you revisit all the fights that were clearly instigated by your ex.

Observe how quickly, how automatically, comes your response. See how it seems to be practically *inherent* to the thing itself—almost as though the event and its effect on you were all of a piece. There's no awareness of a moment of choice to think or feel a certain way. See how it's taken for granted that the objective reality has *caused* what's become your inner reality.

How hard it is to imagine it could be otherwise—that the thing could happen and yet you have a different, milder, more matter-of-fact response. The outward reality would be its same self, yet there wouldn't be the gathering of bile, the stomach-twisting, the obsessive thoughts running away with themselves. Take it further: see how difficult it is to imagine (truly radical) *no response at all*. The real-life thing could be as it is, yet you're in no way stirred up inside.

There's no need to rush to that possibility as a goal. The absence of thought and emotion isn't necessarily desirable as a uniform orientation to life events. Its potential is being introduced to help you realize something: that your inner response to a thing is *entirely independent* of the thing itself. The real occurrence has its self-contained existence, prior to what you make of it. So truly is this so that (yes) it's conceivable that you could encounter something, even something fairly big, wholly taking in its factuality, *without ever deciding what you think or feel about it.*

Outer reality is one thing and your response is another. Mostly, this is not a welcome thing to see. Because the experience most of the time is that inner option is not in the picture. "I can't help it," a person will say. And truly, that is the experience, on the level of feeling: as life is lived and felt, the outer thing appears to cause, as if inevitably, the inner orientation to it.

This isn't a suggestion that you try to force yourself to see it differently. That's not the way change takes place—by *installing* an idea, force-feeding it to yourself. Doing that is nothing but a setup to encourage you to lie to yourself about your feelings, or a breeding ground for discouragement or anger over the suggestion that you have control over the extent to which you suffer, when you do not—yet—experience the truth of that.

Simply pay attention to the way it functions *now.* Watch how things influence your interior. In a moment-to-moment way, do this. Not in a big-picture way. Just now, and now. Observe how fast the reaction comes, the appearance of a causal relationship between outer and inner.

Notice the relationship between thought and emotion. When a potent emotion comes alive, look *behind* it for a thought that is the source of its vitality. The thought is the power supply. If that prior thought had been somehow otherwise, the resultant emotion would also be different. The event (apparently) "caused" the thought, and the thought (actually) caused the emotion.

Say you learn you're being laid off. After the initial moments of taking in the news of this unanticipated development, you begin thinking about how hard you've worked at the job, how unappreciated you've been by your boss and coworkers. The more you revisit your history there, the more resentful you feel. You begin to stew, mentally rehearsing things you'll say to your boss, thinking how good it will feel to get it all off your chest, with nothing now to lose.

Alternatively, say you got the same piece of news. You realize—*Well, I haven't actually been content in this job for some time now.* You start considering what other sorts of work might better suit you. You begin to feel a surge of energy for launching out, exploring new possibilities. Not a situation you'd have chosen, but it does feel like a fresh start. Your spirits lift.

In each case, the mood you end up in was set in motion by the thing your mind did with the news. You probably didn't experience a moment of choosing to start up one story versus the other. Nevertheless, the story you settled on is what gave rise to the mental/emotional reality you're now living with.

Don't attempt to force an alternative thought onto the inner mind screen. The idea isn't to try to start up a positive story. It's to see that *some* story does start up—and to see how it determines the way you feel. You can't make yourself change by pushing a negative response under water. Simply see what's happening.

Nothing about this can be hurried or artificial. You'll experience the distinctness of inner and outer only over time, as a natural outcome of observing how it is now.

Feel how challenging it is to allow yourself to be where you are, especially in the heat of a real situation. What courage it takes to accept what's really happening inside, in an open-eyed, unresisting way. Allow yourself to feel the force of the "automatic" thoughts and emotions, the speed with which it all takes place, as though you have no say in what's happening. How directly and forcefully the outer thing appears to result in the inner situation. Just see it, without trying to change it.

But you surely will change. *If you're willing to see where you are.* Carry a background awareness that it could be otherwise.

You are ready to entertain this possibility, however implausible it might now seem, or you wouldn't be here.

Two Distinct Things

However little you may experience it, in a given moment, choice is in fact operating. The ego-mind, being a profoundly self-serving entity, cannot be trusted to provide a reliable accounting of the truth. It's in the ego's self-interest to believe that life-stuff is entirely responsible for how things feel within.

The prison cell comes from seeing as a single thing what are really two. We are trapped only as long as we believe ourselves to be.

Remember that an awake person experiences equanimity in the presence of even a huge external uproar. Inner and outer reality are entirely disconnected, with the experience of choice being constantly alive, readily exercised. Which is why it's possible to experience sustained peace even in a world brimming with suffering and injustice. Remember too that the reason enduring awakeness so seldom occurs is exactly *because* it flies in the face of the ego's impression of truth.

What you're trying to discover here is how choice *already* operates. Even if you're not able to actually choose differently, you might sometimes see how your egoic self benefits from a given inner reaction, even when the thoughts and emotions are uncomfortable. Perhaps it gives you an impression of control; maybe it supports a sense of yourself that you've long identified with (and wouldn't readily dis-identify from). The ego's primary concern is keeping itself going, even at the cost of diving head-first into anguish.

You may come to see that in some way it serves you (your ego-mind) to believe you *can't help it*. If you're truthful with yourself, you'll occasionally realize that, deeply, you do not *want to believe* choice is being exercised. There may be moments of seeing that you *do* choose to think certain thoughts, because you notice a shift from one interpretation to a different one, resulting in changed emotions.

Choice always has been operating, but you didn't see it. You've been heavily invested in *not* seeing it. Because if you recognized choice at play, you would reasonably exercise it—or else acknowledge that you're heading wide-eyed into suffering. No one would choose pain understood to be optional. It's easier, more bearable, to throw up your hands and declare yourself at the mercy of forces beyond your control.

You might say you know about the distinctness of external reality from what you make of it. But this "knowing" may be conceptual only. Viscerally recognizing choice when it flowers in a real-life episode is another thing altogether. What the mind has learned about choice can be remote at such a moment.

It may be awhile before you're able to exercise conscious choice in your mental/emotional state. But paying attention at moments of apparent causation prepares the ground for eventual change in that direction. You're seeing that suffering has something to do with what you tell yourself about the occurrence—that reality alone isn't entirely responsible.

Simply doing this nonjudgmental seeing may actually quiet the uproar somewhat, because the act of bringing awareness into the picture gives you a sense that not all of you is affected. Noticing yourself react shifts you slightly outside the uproar. Watching, you aren't fully identified with the reaction. The real-seemingness of the mind-produced version of things is compromised by gently "staring it down." You may feel less at the mercy of reality, with an easing of discomfort.

Occupying the Gap

Although the gap between inner and outer is experienced in time (because it comes *after* the real-life occurrence and *before* any response), the sensation is like slipping into a space. A breathing space, a break in the action, where you can look at the situation, without unconsciously racing ahead in pure egoic reactivity. It is wildly liberating to find that space.

Finding the gap has value beyond creating space to think clearly and respond deliberately. Aware of the situation but not caught up in it, you may sense the living presence of your higher self, the "you" not caught in the machinery of the torment-producing mind. You get to experience that there's more to you than your ego-mind. The place you're watching *from* is located outside the fray.

Remember: this awareness is no finger-wagging task master. It's not the same thing as embarrassed self-consciousness. It wants nothing to be different from what it is. Like a camera lens, it just *sees*.

Nothing need be done but simple observation. (What a relief, after all the years of self-castigation, the arduous effort to improve yourself!) No resolution to do better. No temptation to lie to yourself about how you're really doing. Once the radical distinctness of cause from its apparent effect is seen, the rest takes care of itself. The possibility of choice begins to flower.

When the higher awareness comes alive, in a moment of anxiety or anger or humiliation—when you neutrally see yourself in the scene—*notice what the looking feels like*. Acknowledge the calm presence of the looker. The outer situation is here; your mind may still be producing thoughts, resulting in emotional upset. Yet *something real in you* is able to observe it all happening. The more you sense the presence of this observer, the more likely you are to get (*viscerally*, not conceptually) that option is operating.

Both are innate to your humanity: the egoic self that believes itself to be at the mercy of life, and (right beside it) an awareness that knows better. Note that the one self doesn't talk to the other. The watcher knows better than to expect to influence the ego-mind, which believes entirely in the necessity of the ruckus and discounts that there's any more to you than itself.

How Suffering Begins to Abate

How does occupying that vantage point outside the drama eventually reduce suffering?

Simply from the gently cultivated habit of observing self-in-scene, you're likely to discover that something is shifting. An episode of reality may occur that historically would have set you off, and yet the first thing you'll sense in response will be *not* a mental/emotional reaction, but (such a surprise) the presence of that alive, intelligent alertness.

A blessed pause, where all that's going on is pure attention. No knee-jerk reaction, inside or out. Just a stillness. Within it, the flowering of an unaccustomed freedom: the living reality of choice. To think one thing or a different thing.

Or a true miracle—to think *no thought at all*. Just awareness of what-is. And there you are, fully present for it, in the direct encounter with reality. No uproar. Eyes wide open.

You'll find, over time, that there's more to say in the matter of how you're doing than you ever imagined, no matter what life brings you. You'll learn you don't have to be a passive victim of life. *The power of reality to determine your state of mind is a power that you give it.* You could decline to give it that control. You cannot see the one thing without also seeing the other.

The spiritual life is about learning how to be fundamentally okay no matter what happens. It's about relaxing the dogged attempt to fix each thing as it comes along, instead putting primary attention on your interior. This isn't about keeping a stiff upper lip, or living at a distance from life, or taking refuge in comforting ideas about how "none of this is real." It's about being in full recognition of what-is, even as you're not at its mercy.

Be alert to thoughts like these: *I can't possibly be serene, with all I'm facing. People who seem okay no matter what must be in major denial.* Behind this thinking is the persistent belief that life really is in charge of a person's inner state.

Life will never stop being itself. It won't come to a point where everything evens out for keeps. Change is ceaseless, with precious little there's any hope of controlling. Decay is inevitable. You've spent your whole life (so far) putting out fires, swinging at pitched balls, cutting your losses, working on yourself, rearranging the furniture (the partner, the job, the appearance). All so you could be okay inside. It's always looked as though contentment required something of your circumstances. Something in you (in everyone) clings to the idea that first you just need to get the big things right, and *then* you can find your way to peace and fulfillment. Or if you can just hang on till retirement, things will be better.

It's a stunning proposition: that you don't need to straighten things out first, before getting down to being happy.

We're taught to believe that joy and lightness of heart are *caused* by something—usually something external to ourselves—and that deep fulfillment comes of accomplishing something. The task is not to fix life. The task is to see how outer reality holds a flute to its lips and you dance to its tune.

Eventually, you can get to where life is allowed to simply be itself. You take action where action is called for, but it isn't driven by some overwhelming force inside. You experience a steady peacefulness that doesn't waver in the presence of difficulty.

Disconnecting the wiring of reactivity doesn't only diminish suffering. It also helps you see that the *you* that's done the reacting isn't who you most deeply are. What a revelation. You may find you're living more in the steady awareness of you-*as-awareness-itself*—not as the ego-mind that's subject to the push and pull of life.

A New Groove

I remember vividly what it felt like being the center of my world, the magnetic center of awareness, everything in relation to me. Being in any situation meant I felt something about it: liked it, disdained it; felt bored with it, scared of it; hoped it would last, wished to escape it.

Once, some years ago, this oddball thought came to me. From out of the blue, it just arrived. I hadn't been thinking about things—at least, not things like this. I was lying in the bathtub at the time.

You know how when you realize something big, you're likely to always remember where you were when it happened?

This was the thought: What I *feel* about something isn't the most important thing.

I could see this was hitting me pretty hard. I thought—*Okay, what's the big deal here? Why is this making such an impression?* My mind kept turning over the idea, as it would examine any novel thing. It was like the thought was cutting a new groove in my head.

It would be a long time before I'd appreciate the fullness of what came to me that day.

I couldn't have had that thought if I didn't realize (even if unconsciously) that whatever I felt about something *was* the most important thing. Up until that moment in the bathtub, anyhow. It had been that way my entire forty-some-year-old life.

Life consisted of moving along from caring about one thing to caring about the next, and the next, with the prospect of it going that way to the end of time (*my* time). This was the stream of my inner life: care about whether my kids got off to school on time, about the political situation, about what somebody said or did. Everything was about how it affected me, how it "made me feel." How I thought about it, how I talked about it, what I did about it.

I never questioned this, or even saw that it was going on. I took it that much for granted—the necessity of the ongoing "meta-reality" assembled from my impressions of things. I never saw that I was living at a remove from reality, that I was inhabiting not my life but my mind-made picture of it.

When that shock of a thought came to me—*What I feel about a thing isn't what matters most*—it was the door opening on something truly transformative: that it's possible for a thing to simply be itself. That *the thing itself* must have a reality independent of my thinking or feeling anything about it.

Which meant (if the logic was followed through) that there wasn't any compelling necessity for me to be affected. It must be possible to be in life, to be in the presence of one thing and another, without automatically, by some crippling kind of default, having my inner state be determined by it.

If there *were* an inner response, the outer thing would *still be itself*, independent of whatever I made of it.

Only in retrospect, long after life was actually happening in that steadily "unaffected" way, did I understand the significance of that moment in the bathtub—did I see how something began there.

A Project for One (Whole) Day

There's a fun thing you could do that would teach you a lot about yourself—a perspective to adopt for an entire day. *Fun* is the operative word. Because normally this kind of inquiry invites deadly seriousness. Especially if you're hoping to improve, in some way. Or if you think of yourself as a seeker.

Take on this project with a lightness of heart, with the bemused eye of the curious scientist bent on discovery. After all, the whole point of the spiritual life is to end up where you no longer take yourself seriously. If you go about this self-observation with grim determination and guilty recognition of your imperfections, you're only feeding the already ravenous maw of self-importance.

So lighten up. Be willing to look at yourself, but turn off the judging function. This is not about psychoanalyzing yourself, or justifying your foibles. It's not meant to be preparatory to improving yourself. If doing this exercise brings about change, that will happen quite naturally, all on its own.

Even if you think you know yourself well, this exploration may be revelatory. You may have lived for decades, done a lot of spiritual inquiry, worked on yourself in multiple ways. Still, you may be in for a surprise.

For one whole day, notice whenever something gives you a good feeling. Pay attention to even the subtle good-feeling things (including those that strike you as embarrassingly trivial). See if you can sustain the awareness throughout the entire day.

You might reflect ahead of time on the types of things that could stir a good feeling in the course of a typical day. Doing this ahead-of-time reflection can help you recognize the pleasant sensation when it comes.

Things go the way you hoped they would. Somebody says something nice about you. The light turns green just before you get to it. You weigh yourself and see you've lost a pound. Something you worked hard on turns out well. You get through your whole list. You find out you have a buyer for your house, or enough students to make a go of the class you've been hoping to teach. You finish a project you've been working on. The doctor calls and says you don't, after all, have a staph infection. You're finally able to get the lawn mower working. Your partner looks you adoringly in the eye and tells you how wonderful you are.

Your lost cat comes home. You get an email saying your story has been accepted for publication. Your car repair ends up being less expensive than you'd feared. On the radio, you hear that your guy won the election. You narrowly miss getting rear-ended. You've come to the end of your work week and can now relax. You look outside and see it's finally stopped raining. Your therapist says you've made a breakthrough. Your boss gives you a raise. You make a sarcastic remark at a business meeting that elicits laughter.

Your own list is probably already generating itself.

Pick a day that hasn't started yet (how about tomorrow?) and watch yourself move through the day's developments, noticing every time something "makes" you feel even slightly good. The point of doing this isn't to be hard on yourself. It's simply to see what a source of sustenance it all is, in the experience of how-life-is-going.

You're likely to also observe, as you move through the day, those things (small and large) that "make" you feel bad. You could take a separate day for that project. Or, if you can stand the repeated whiplash, do them both on the same day.

You'll see yourself mostly do one of two things with anything significant. If you like it, you'll put your arms around it, taking it along with you in your travels, so you can revisit it later as something you can feel good about. If you don't like it, you'll complain about it, make up dismissive stories about it, justify why things went badly.

The goal isn't to make yourself stop feeling good when good things happen. It's just to see how your underlying sense of well-being is susceptible to how things go.

Don't bother judging yourself for the trivial nature of some of what you discover. The point is to stop taking yourself seriously. But while self-castigation about the particulars is a waste of time, the larger phenomenon is very much worth paying attention to. Remember, it's *human nature* you're learning about here, not your individual neuroses.

Observe how readily your mood is altered by something "out there." See if you can watch it happening without completely buying into the mood (lousy, euphoric, frustrated, gratified). Observe the phenomenon *without losing track of its being a phenomenon.*

In a vivid moment of noticing, ask *What is here that's capable of noticing this?* In a way, that's the entire point of this exercise: not to try to change what you feel, but simply to feel what it's like to get *outside* of it. To experience the presence of the *you* that's not caught up in liking and not-liking. What's valuable is the ability to adopt a perspective different from the usual one.

Perspective, in this business, is everything.

If embarrassment or self-chastisement starts up, you can be sure it's a sign you aren't outside of the phenomenon. It's the ego taking you to task. If that happens, take a step to the side and observe the squirmy feeling that's begun to flood you. You're no longer in it.

It's a necessary shock to become acquainted, maybe for the first time, with what's actually driving your sense of how life feels a lot of the time. You're discovering how uphill it is to see through all the reactivity to the moment itself. But the discomfort doesn't last, not if you stay with this process. Little by little, you begin to take your thoughts less seriously. They become features of the landscape, like furniture or trees. Life continues, one event after another, but something in the middle of all the action is beginning to recognize itself. It feels, occasionally, more real than the contents of your head. More real than the you that's having all these opinions.

But then the next thing you know, you're back in it, blaming the outer stuff on how you feel.

Be patient. You didn't form these habits in one day. It will probably take more than a few days for them to undo themselves.

Just keep bringing attention to your interior.

The Big Stuff

Sometimes reality brings you to your knees. Of course a significant loss or challenge is going to cause distress. This pain is not solely mind-generated but is more truly in line with the severity of what life has delivered. If you're awake to reality, you'll feel it all. You'll allow the truth (both the circumstances and your feelings) to have the life it must have.

In working to become more conscious, more alive to reality, the idea is *not* to get to where you'll never hurt again. It's not to imagine you ever could (or should) cultivate an indifference, an aloofness, in dire conditions. It's so you can learn to tell the difference between thought-induced pain and the kind that comes of yielding to a real-life circumstance.

Yet even at such a time, peacefulness needn't be out of the picture.

The ego-mind doesn't want to believe that wholeness and underlying well-being can attend even severe difficulty. It insists, *No, reality really* is *responsible for my inner state. Surely a peaceful condition within is not possible in* this *situation.* Indeed, the egoic self points to this kind of extreme situation to try to make its case.

In a situation of true extremity (clinging to a floating log days after a tsunami, life in a war zone), the requirement to yield can stir a heightened consciousness, summoned by the intensity of the circumstance. A person in such a situation may be shocked to find a profound well-being flooding awareness. Surely a person in such dire straits is not happy. Yet who could be a more compelling authority on the existence of a self that's at the mercy of nothing?

Awakeness doesn't mean uninterrupted happiness. It means uninterrupted *aliveness.* Uninterrupted *peacefulness.* Peacefulness and happiness do not necessarily come as a unit. The reason "the peace that passeth understanding" is hard to wrap the mind around is that it can exist even in the presence of terrible circumstances.

When a hard thing occurs in your life and you don't resist it, and you don't try to reduce it to a collection of thoughts, but instead you're *with* it (including how it hurts), you don't experience being-with-what-is as the familiar kind of suffering. You experience it as aliveness. As life.

And that, whatever life may be delivering at present, is the whole point.

Orientation to the Big Picture

We want to think (we're taught to do so) that the big-picture stuff, the mental understanding of where a person is in life, is always the significant thing to pay attention to. *I can't seem to keep a relationship together. I want my daughter to be happy. I've got to improve my health.* The overall view is where attention will often go, as the default. The ego-mind is accustomed to scanning the landscape (of the day, the week, the time of life, the situation) to see how things are going, what's next, and so on. What's going on *now* can be experienced as an actual distraction from the mind's persistent focus on the life situation.

Yet everything that ever happens is, in fact, lived in some present-tense moment. No matter what the habitually-taken larger view is able to take in, actual experience (awareness, action, feeling, choice) takes place in the present. The present is where you experience your aliveness. It's at enormous cost that present reality is neglected in favor of what the mind ceaselessly re-minds you of.

The reality of the moment is whatever you're able to directly encounter in the immediate scene. It's what's happening *now.* The larger picture requires the use of the mind (to recall or project, since what constitutes the big picture isn't *here now*). That is, you cannot directly experience it this moment, but can encounter it only via thought. Yet sometimes the bigger picture asks for a certain kind of attention.

In present-moment awareness, where can you helpfully locate the big view of things? When you focus on immediate reality, what happens to your grasp of the larger situation?

Being in the moment doesn't mean the context doesn't matter. It's not as though by focusing on the present, you're trying to make yourself forget about your life overall—something pending, unsettled, some ongoing problem needing attention. *There will always be a big picture, if you look for one.* What you're focusing on right now may be naturally informed by whatever your mind is aware of in a background sort of way.

When there's an ongoing situation that's difficult or absorbing, it tends to be taken for granted that it will be "with you," affecting the state of mind and heart, in pretty much of an ongoing way, whether or not something of the situation is actually occurring in the immediate scene. While the mind's ability to visualize the larger picture can be of benefit, it also enables you to fret and obsess—to never be able to rest from an ongoing situation, even when nothing relevant is needing attention in a given moment. It's as if the situation is constantly present. The experience of many an otherwise ordinary moment is colored by the background awareness of the circumstance, because it's "on your mind." The burden of the knowledge is carried— *needlessly*—from moment to moment, the mind ever convincing in its insistence that what's in the big picture needs steady vigilance (as if it will improve things).

If nothing of the big picture is showing up right now, and you can manage to be present with that truth, then you can be relieved (for now, anyhow) of thinking about it. Why not? You probably need all the relief you can get.

You're not being urged to abandon or disregard ongoing issues, goals, developments, nor are you being asked to forget what's going on elsewhere in the world, in other people's lives. Being in the present doesn't ask you to live in disregard of the larger picture. This isn't about doing one to the exclusion of the other. Yet in the vast majority of lives, one happens very much to the exclusion of the other, and at great cost: people tend to live so much in the big-picture "reality" constantly imported by the mind into the present, that they actually miss the present moment itself.

It's possible to live your life with an ongoing *background* awareness of the larger picture while keeping *primary* attention on the immediate.

It's possible to be present with *this* reality, even as the larger situation is known. Often, the life situation is best served by focusing on the now. If you want to improve your health by forgoing certain foods, the best way to accomplish that is not to eat one of them *now.*

The thing to realize, whenever you feel thrown off-balance by mental activity, is that the actual present moment is of a different order of reality from the one your mind presents to you for consideration. Keep reminding yourself there's choice in how you orient yourself to the mind's content.

Two Orders of Reality

When you notice yourself "lost in your head," bring your attention to what's in the immediate scene. Whatever activity or condition is apparent; what your senses perceive; what you're doing; what you feel like physically. Bring the primary focus to the reality of the present moment, even as you're aware of the larger context.

The multifaceted intelligence available to you means it's possible to live in this moment, to feel yourself occupying it, with the ongoing contextual awareness. But it isn't necessary to indulge your mind when it tries to squeeze the entire long-term situation into *this* moment, asking you to orient to it as though it were all real right now.

What might happen later, just as what happened previously, isn't happening now. What's happening elsewhere in the world is not happening here.

People living in circumstances of protracted poverty or chaos, or the ongoing threat of harm, may be aided in their struggle to cope by focusing on the present. Even as there must be the ongoing effort to improve or leave the situation, with whatever available resources and assistance, the panicked anxiety and vigilance that tend to accompany dangerous or desperate circumstances can be eased somewhat by focusing attention on the here and now. Indeed, sometimes that happens automatically, so extreme is the demand of the present moment.

The now and the content of the mind are not of the same order of reality. There's no reason for the mind-generated content to become primary in awareness unless thinking can usefully be applied to it *right now.*

Oh! But (you say) I don't seem to have control over when the mind-generated stuff shows up. Yes, this is the way of it.

You're not being asked to attempt to control what seems to be an overwhelming force. The invitation is simply to observe that the mental "reality" (when it barges in) is on one plane of real while the immediate scene is on another. Learn to stop mixing them up, as though they were all one thing. When you become aware of your interior, in a given moment, see how you can shift your attention from one to the other: from the mental content (whatever it may be, however compelling) to the immediate scene. Then, just to see that you can do it, shift it back again. Notice your feeling state as you bring attention deliberately to the one versus to the other. See how much more peaceful you feel when you allow the focus on mind-made reality to recede in favor of attention on the immediate (*regardless* of what the immediate scene holds, whether or not it looks peace-inducing).

Again and again, come back to this truth: life is actually lived in the present. That has been true your entire life. It will never stop being true.

Getting Help

Adopting a spiritual orientation to life doesn't mean it might not make good sense during difficult times to seek available help. Psychotherapy (perhaps supported by medication) can be a great aid in coping with a challenging situation. It can help you to separate what you have control over from what you do not—to address what can be changed, and to peacefully accept what you have to live with. Therapy that addresses the mind's role in influencing how you feel can be a valuable accompaniment to spiritual inquiry. Getting regular exercise and making lifestyle changes may help unwind the desperation of feeling at the mercy of life developments.

A spiritual life isn't inconsistent with seeking the support or assistance of social service, mental health, or medical professionals, or authorities in the legal and judicial systems, when these are called for.

10

Acceptance: Unplugging the Suffering Machine

Here is a formula for misery: resist a fact. Lament something that has occurred, dwelling on how it could have been otherwise.

If you were to altogether let go of resistance this moment, never to start it up again, by that single gesture, you'd liberate yourself from an enormous burden of suffering. Whatever time remains would feel conspicuously different from all that has preceded.

Allowing reality to be itself means you no longer blame life for your inner condition—or credit it, if things are going well. The potential exists to be at peace *no matter what.*

Confronted with reality, there are two options. You can acknowledge the fact of it, without resistance, or you can argue with it. When you oppose reality in any way, you're taking on a terrible weight, which you then carry. It becomes a part of you. The burden wears you out.

The alternative is to directly look at what's real, now. To stand in its presence, in full, unresisting recognition. To let the *fact* of it be primary, prior to everything else, like how you feel about it, or whether you might want to take action.

When you accept, you align all of attention with what's here. You are literally *one* with it. There's no perception of distance from the real, no room for resistance. Only when you distance yourself from reality does it become possible to reject it, to disapprove (or approve) of it. If feelings are stirred by what's happening, you yield to that inner reality too. It's all in the picture of what's real.

When your primary sense of a thing is its factuality, the attention of the higher self is engaged. But when the focus is on *your orientation* to it, your familiar-self awareness is in charge. The ego-mind is trying to inject something of itself into outer reality—to project a positive or negative value, some kind of label—which is different from just letting it be what it is.

Resistance versus acceptance has everything to do with which "one" of you is showing up. The choice determines whether the machinery of suffering starts up or is allowed to remain at rest.

Your higher self does not suffer. Your familiar self can hardly figure out how *not* to suffer.

The Experience of Resisting

Resisting is a tensing-against something. It gets revved up via some kind of mental handling (complaint, story-spinning, denial), leading to emotional distress. Whatever difficulty you're experiencing in the presence of something you'd prefer hadn't happened, resistance compounds the challenge by piling on negativity. It heaps suffering on top of suffering, intensifying the pain of what's already hurting. Pushing against something that's insisting its presence into your life involves pointless exertion. It's tiring.

If you tense your arm for an injection, it hurts more.

At a time of challenge, you need to save your valuable resources for addressing the situation. If you wear yourself out in anger or denial, if you allow yourself to get stuck in the past (how the situation could have been avoided or foreseen), there won't be as much positive energy and creativity available to do something useful to improve things. To move on from here.

Before fruitful moving-on can take place, *here* has to be seen for what it is. It has to be allowed.

Acceptance Is Not Approval

Allowing the fact of a thing has nothing to do with liking it. Having wanted something to be otherwise pales beside the truth that *it happened the way it did*. Understanding the power of acceptance means realizing this essential truth.

This isn't about putting a good spin on something unwelcome. Acceptance has nothing to do with a positive orientation. It's also not about being a doormat.

We tend to think that acceptance is tantamount to approval. That resistance is justified (even inevitable) if a thing is deemed unfavorable. These beliefs suggest it isn't possible to accept something you wish were otherwise. They locate the cause of suffering in the wrong place, attaching it to the outer development, instead of pointing at the resistance.

Another erroneous assumption has to do with the desire for change. Accepting something doesn't mean you're stuck with it, if it's amenable to improvement. You can accept reality and then move on to trying to bring about change. It's often supposed that corrective action must begin with railing against what is. Political action is typically fueled by forceful opposition (even anger and hatred) against those who see things another way. The truth is, resistance brews only negativity. Whether you want to get your candidate elected or dig your car out of a snow bank, indignation is a drain, not a positive force. Work for change that starts with resistance of the current situation is a breeding ground for recklessness and squandered resources. When anger, frustration, and judgment spur action to right a perceived wrong, as much harm is done as good.

The effort will be both more productive and more pleasant if it's launched from a calm acceptance of the present situation. Seeing where things *are* establishes a tone of receptivity and openness. Intelligence, creativity, and devotion thrive in an environment of acceptance. The desired outcome grows more likely. Meanwhile, suffering isn't compounded by negativity.

Being Sane

When you allow intelligent awareness to take in reality and say *this is what's real,* something in you feels sane. A feeling of craziness comes about when you get stuck in insisting that this (actual, real) thing should be different from what it is—that it shouldn't have happened. *But it did.* There's a conflict between the intelligence that sees truth and the ego that dislikes it. Peace becomes impossible.

The ego-mind insists that its annoyance/disappointment/indignation can somehow overwhelm reality. Meanwhile, a deeper knowing sees the absurdity of the attempt to vanquish what-is. The pain of resistance comes of investing in what's deeply known to be madness: the effort to undo what cannot be undone.

When you turn *toward* something difficult, when you allow yourself to be sane, you ease into peacefulness. You couldn't do a kinder thing for yourself.

Noticing Resistance

It's one thing for the mind to be persuaded of the sanity of acceptance, in the abstract, and quite another to actually accept an unwelcome real-life development.

If you're driving along and flashing blue lights show up in your rear view mirror, it's inevitable you'll tighten against the prospect of getting a ticket—isn't it? If you spill coffee on your tan pants while rushing out the door to go to work, it seems natural you'll be irritated (you don't have any other clean pants, plus now you'll be late). How could it be otherwise?

The reaction seems inherent to what's happened. Resistance comes very fast.

Maybe it's true you just wrecked your good pants, and you're going to be late to work. Maybe you *are* about to get a ticket. But cursing at these things will do nothing to make them untrue. All it does is worsen an already miserable moment.

Here's where bringing attention to awareness, in a moment of life, bears fruit. Seeing what you're feeling highlights what you have to say in the matter of whether (and how much) you suffer. Self-observation is the effective teacher—and it goes with you everywhere you go, if you remember to allow it.

The beginning of the discovery is noticing when resistance starts. A clue that you're pushing against reality will likely be some kind of inner disturbance. Anytime you feel discomfort or negativity within, look to see if there's something you're resisting. The early signs are often felt in the body: muscular tension, facial expression, eyes rolling up in the head, a dismissive gesture of the hands, the whole body turning away. Meanwhile, the mind starts its commentary. *This is ridiculous! I should've been more careful. Look at that idiot.* As resistance ripens, strong emotions may be generated (fury, dread, frustration). You may find you're working to avoid feelings, to squash them under the pressure of the mind's monologue. If someone else is there, chances are you'll vent, raise your voice, attempt to engage the other in negativity. Maybe you'll deny the situation, trying to escape it, physically or mentally.

As you become aware of resisting, note that the cause of discomfort isn't entirely the outer situation. Sometimes seeing the pain generated by resistance will cause it to dissipate. Even if the resistance continues, noticing the sensation of pushing against the unwelcome thing will benefit you. Over multiple episodes, you'll see how fighting reality actually causes pain. Eventually, you're sure to become better able to accept what you find unpleasant or difficult. You'll suffer less, simply because of having given attention to what resistance feels like in real-life experience.

Ordinary life delivers up a steady stream of things we could do without. Whether it's something trivial (the car not starting) or major (the marriage breaking up), the machinery of resistance is the same. If you've done the day-long observation of good/bad feelings, you may have noticed that the initial response to disliked things involved resistance. (If you haven't done this exercise yet, you'll find it illuminates the connection between resistance and suffering.)

Once you get that reality simply *is* (whether or not you'd have chosen it), you've taken a significant step away from being at the mercy of life. When you stop needing to know whether a given experience is friend or foe, you have a taste of freedom.

Life provides abundant opportunities to yield to unwelcome reality. Most are declined, quite automatically, without questioning. As your willingness to notice yourself becomes steady, things that could be yielded to will be recognized and turned toward, sparing you the pain of resistance.

You'll discover choice where you never imagined it could be.

The Anatomy of Resistance

One afternoon on your way home from work, you're talking on your cell phone. Distracted, you don't see a board lying in the road in time to steer around it. It occurs to you there might have been a nail in it, that you should remember to check your tires when you get home. By the time you roll into your driveway, you've forgotten, fixated on removing your uncomfortable shoes and getting a bite to eat.

The next morning, when you go out to head to work, you see you have a flat. What's your reaction? A choice word or two muttered to yourself. A stomp in the dirt beside the car, or (better) a swift kick to the deflated rubber. *I should've remembered to check when I got home. I shouldn't talk on the phone while I'm driving. Damn whoever dropped that board in the road.* Now you're going to be late. The entire time you're jacking up the car and fighting with the lug nuts, you're fuming—at the expense of the new tire you may have to buy, at your job that you hate, at yourself for your carelessness.

It doesn't look as though any of it could be any other way. If some smiling person were to walk onto the scene saying, "Relax, just change the tire," you'd snarl.

But slow the whole thing down. Take it apart, frame by frame, and look at what happened. You saw the tire was flat, and before you could move on to frustration and anger, something had to say, *This shouldn't have happened.*

But it did.

That intermediary step—the lightning-fast resistance—is what enables negativity to blossom. That in-between tightening is the quietly beating heart that keeps alive a great deal of misery.

You'd swear the cause of your irritation is the flat tire. But the real culprit is the failure to accept.

When you say *this shouldn't have happened,* what you're attempting to do is go back in time—to *undo reality.* How different you'd feel if instead of rushing to react, you just took a moment to let the fact sink in. Anything that could have prevented this situation is beyond your reach. It's a sublime waste of time and energy to go back in your mind. Nothing in your head can change how flat the tire is. Nothing alters the fact that you've got to do something to fix it.

Acceptance is a show-stopper. When you accept that the tire is flat, you skip the self-induced misery and get on with being practical. You become efficient, resourceful, instead of flying into a fit and making mistakes, doing more damage. Hurting yourself by rushing, being careless with the jack. Neglecting to tighten the lugs because instead of focusing on what you're doing, you're obsessively reliving the moment of rolling over the board.

Peacefulness comes from allowing what-is to fully penetrate, without escaping into your head to start a story about how it could have been otherwise, or wondering how much worse things might get.

If it's something big you're yielding to, acceptance can feel like holding still for the sharp edge of a knife blade. But then you can effectively move on to what's next. Allowing a painful reality is vastly preferable to becoming paralyzed by the refusal to acknowledge the truth.

Accepting something doesn't require you to spin a supporting narrative about why it happened, or how it's "a blessing in disguise." The mental activity is the ego's attempt to make palatable something you wish hadn't happened. Skip it. Just see the thing for what it is, and get on with what's next.

Shocked, Surprised, Startled: Discovering Expectation (After the Fact)

Sometimes a teacher shows up in the most unexpected places.

You get into your car and slide the key into the ignition, and when you turn it you're greeted with a stunning silence. Something in you registers surprise (and probably dismay). It's not until that instant that you realize (if you think to go looking) that you opened the car door with the unconscious expectation that the engine would start, as it has virtually every time prior.

Midway through the first semester of your son's senior year of college, and him just accepted for graduate school abroad, you're in the midst of renovating his bedroom into an office for the home-based business you're about to launch. For some years, you've looked forward to this moment of starting a new venture, after years of active parenthood. One evening, as you're moving a filing cabinet into your office, your son calls and announces he's dropping out of college. He's realized the career path he's been headed toward is just not for him. He sounds distressed and anxious, and says he wants to live at home for a while so he can take some time to sort out what's next for him.

You sure had been looking forward to that empty nest.

In the effort to reduce the suffering caused by resistance, there's no necessity to somehow keep yourself from supposing things will go the expected way. You don't have to cultivate an artificial "negative expectation" about everyday things having high reliability—to orient yourself to your car in such a way that you "expect" it equally to start and not to start on any given attempt with the key.

Just the same, it's useful to notice the moments when an expectation is dashed, to see the habitual assumption that things will go according to plan. It can be eye-opening to explore how the unconscious assumption interferes with presence, the ability to accept whatever comes.

There's seldom reason to notice, but you go around all day with a huge number of unseen expectations running in the background of all you do. The car will start, the computer will boot, you won't spill your drink, nothing will break or be lost, scheduled things will happen, unscheduled things will not. You will not have a car accident or come down with a sickness, your partner won't leave you, jets will not fly into the World Trade Center.

The primary expectation, of course, is this one: "This time tomorrow, I will still be alive." (All others are riding on that one.)

That things have always (or mostly) gone a certain way naturally gives rise to the expectation that they will continue to do so. We want to be able to assume that things set in motion will unfold as intended. We count on laws, systems, customs, schedules, and actuarial tables to assert control and predictability in a world where chaos and change are powerful players. In the context of uncertainty, anything predictive generates a comforting sense of *the known*, so that at least some of life feels reliable. Which is to say, safe.

Anything we normally count upon that suddenly proves unreliable is unnerving. We get disoriented, frightened, irritated. Resistant.

Living alongside all the underground expectations that keep us feeling roughly okay is the knowledge that at least once in a while something somewhere *won't* go as expected. There's no telling which corner it's hiding around, or under which pile of leaves it's concealed (grenade-like), and what form it will take is anybody's guess. So, for many, the radar of vigilance is constantly turned on, scanning the landscape, hoping against hope that things will hold for the next few weeks, or at least long enough to get a decent night's sleep. Whenever something goes as expected (the engine roars into action when the key is turned, the plane lands safely), there's a subtle relief, a vague reassurance that *something* is within control. Something that *could* have gone wrong did not.

A lot of the amorphous anxiety that attends modern life comes from the deeply buried coexistence of two things: the knowledge that nothing can ultimately be counted upon, and the ceaseless search (known to be futile) for something ultimately reliable. Even with something as trivial as spilled coffee, the startled reaction contains an element of the frustrated ongoing struggle to have control.

When something startles or surprises you, you couldn't have been caught off-guard without some prior expectation that things would go a certain way. That is where the teacher is: in that moment of recognition. It's not likely you'll stop having the initial knee-jerk reaction, when something comes from out of the blue. But pausing a moment, in the immediate aftermath, to reflect on the ongoing tendency to anticipate sameness, to take habitual comfort in the predictable, can make it easier to *accept* something unexpected (if not this time, maybe next). It can help you move on from this point with relative equanimity.

This reflection also enables an attunement to the subtle presence of expectation running when nothing surprising happens, while things are roughly stable, going along as usual. You see yourself assuming you know how things will be. Sensing that assumption of predictability, you may be able to release the subtle tension of anxious vigilance associated with uncertainty. You may be able to let go of any anticipation at all, slipping (surprise!) into *this very moment*, with no spare attention misspent on thinking you can know what's ahead.

Imagine what it would be like to live without any expectation at all: either that things will go a certain way, or that they won't . . . or that *you* will even continue. What would this moment feel like? How would you occupy the *now* if there were no expectation at all in its atmosphere?

You can discover how expectation runs your life if you observe just two tendencies: how often resistance starts up, and how prone you are to being startled. Startling happens when you're expecting the status quo to hold: the silence to sustain; the ground ahead of your feet to remain level and free of obstruction; the traffic all around you to flow in the accustomed lawful pattern; the bottle on the refrigerator shelf to remain upright.

Watching Change Happen

The habit of resistance won't undo itself in a week. It will take some time, many episodes of resistance starting up, followed by your noticing it's happening, followed by your . . . either egging it on, or gently opening to accept what you've initially fought.

When resistance is felt and allowed to relax, you sense the subtle presence of ease. See that the source of peace is *within*— not in outer reality. Nothing factual, after all, has changed. The simple gesture of being with what-is brings you into the present. This is where you experience your aliveness. Resistance robs you of presence by shutting down attention and driving you into your head, where you become at the mercy of one frustrated thought after another. As soon as you turn toward what you've been resisting, peace has an open door to enter through.

When you are receptive, life is experienced as soft, even when misfortune comes along. The challenge is less daunting when you don't meet it with rigidity. The space that once would have been muddied by frustration and denial is given to pure attention. There's nothing left over to wish the thing hadn't happened.

It's as though you're bowing to reality. A bow is a nod, a full-bodied way of saying, *Yes, it is so.*

The Secret to a Peaceful Life

The usual approach to cultivating peace is to try to establish particular conditions. The assumption is that in order to feel peaceful, you must have the right circumstances, perhaps having to do with stability, safety, or calm. It's supposed that peacefulness has something to do with the big picture.

In fact, peace is momentary. It's only *here and now* that you can feel peaceful (or anything at all), because only the present is real, or ever will be. Any impression of "situational" peacefulness exists in the mind, a thought about what might constitute a setup for peace. The actual *experience* of well-being occurs in a living moment. Nothing is experienced situationally.

The belief that things must be a certain way for you to feel at peace assumes there's a necessary connection between the outer situation and your inner state. Yet it's entirely possible to be in apparently peace-inducing circumstances while being deeply tormented. You can be in a chaotic, noisy, dangerous setting, yet be deeply at ease (even as you're aware of what's around you).

Whatever the circumstances, the experience of peacefulness will *always* come down to how *this moment* feels.

The attempt to arrange circumstances as a way to ensure peace is doomed not to eliminate uncertainty and anxiety, but to generate more of them. Chaos and change will always be at least potentially in the picture, so there can be no reliable stability. Though we secretly know this to be true, we are reluctant to admit it.

While the idea of a peaceful life is an elusive dream, a peaceful *moment* is constantly attainable. Bring attention to what's here and now, without resistance of what's happening—not what's happening *nowadays* or in the larger picture, but just here, now. Peacefulness comes with unresisting attention. As soon as thought starts up with an opinion or a worry, peace flies off like a frightened bird. Thinking is often a counter force to peace, especially when reality is difficult.

A Challenging Situation Lived in the Moment

Not resisting a flat tire or spilled coffee asks for a yielding that's moderately challenging. But these are trivial episodes, time-limited and without lasting impact. What about when you're presented with a life-altering development that won't readily resolve, like a serious diagnosis, your house burning to the ground, the death of a family member? How does nonresistance function in that kind of context?

When you're asked to bow to something daunting, the emotions are likely to be overwhelming. Make no attempt to subdue or escape the painful feelings that come. Yielding to your inner reality is the surest way to "get through your head" the truth of what's come into your life. You may go through this a number of times, as feelings arise and subside. Incorporating a devastating truth can mean multiple confrontations, asking again and again for an open, unresisting heart.

In a situation like this—the larger truth of which can be too much to hold, to accept—it can be a blessing to remember that it's only *this moment* you must be with, even as you're aware of the big picture, and its ramifications are known to reach beyond the present. What's unbearable on the comprehensive scale can be manageable when you ask, *What of the situation is here right now?*

The present moment is not only the only one you *need* to be with; it's also the only one you *can* accept, in any real way. When your mind asks you to surrender to the entire situation, it's trying to take on a task that's literally impossible. It's telling you to accept *in advance* multiple (maybe countless) difficult moments. What has not come yet *is not real* and so cannot be accepted (or resisted!). What the mind projects ahead to and asks you to accept as *real* is a thought only. This is the case even if you're able to predict with a high degree of certainty what the future will hold.

For the larger situation to be brought into present-moment awareness, the *mind* must be engaged. When instead your *attention* is brought to focus on what's immediate, your mind resting from extending further out, you're likely to find nonresistance more doable. The attempt to accept a thing in the future can mislead you into supposing you're ready for something you cannot really prepare yourself for ahead of time. Even if you could somehow accept in advance, *you'd have to do it all over again when it became actual.*

Another aid to managing a severe challenge is to see if there's action that might be taken. After taking in the truth of what can *only* be accepted, do what can be done to help the situation, if there is anything.

If you learn you have a serious illness, first you must take in the difficult news. Each time you remember what you're facing, allow the painful feelings to come. You may believe you could have prevented this situation, by having a healthier lifestyle . . . but that isn't what happened. To the extent that you can spare yourself living in the past (including a past that didn't happen), you'll be better able to surrender to the present. The sooner you accept your condition, the sooner you'll be able to come to some measure of peace, and to move forward with taking whatever helpful action there is. You cannot undo the diagnosis, but you can look into treatment methods. You can see if you want to make changes in your habits. If you've been told there's nothing to be done, you can rest from wishing there were. Just live, one moment at a time— which always was the only way living could be done.

In the case of being with acute or chronic physical pain, along with taking any available steps to ease the discomfort, bringing conscious attention into the picture can be a blessed aid in making the discomfort bearable. Do not resist the pain (it only intensifies and extends the misery), and remember that you have only to surrender to what your body feels *right now.* It's only when your mind introduces the picture of pain extending out into the unmeasurable, unpredictable future that yielding becomes unbearable. Even if your mind knows there's more to come (possibly with no end in sight), future moments are not here now. Manage what you can—what's here to be managed.

The Death of a Loved One

When someone beloved has died, the grief can be so powerful that you may fear you simply cannot bear surrendering to the full force of it. Yet holding back from that terrible yielding is not really protecting you so much as it's compounding the suffering. Painful as it is to acknowledge the enormity of the loss, turning toward grief is turning toward love—the love for the person *and* the love that's the nature of unresisting presence. Grief is a potent invitation to profound surrender. When nothing is held back, the surrender to sorrow can summon the deep stillness of presence, an awareness of the larger reality in which all of this is held: the passing of a life, the utter finality of the opportunity to love, the grief that holds you in its grip. In the very moment grief is keenest, you may sense the peaceful presence of all-that-is, and know that it is within you.

As you confront the hard reality of someone's death, it will help to remember that you need accept only *this moment's* loneliness and sadness. The succession of hours and days and months ahead will arrive, each in its own time, and you will be with each one *then,* as it comes.

Accepting the passing of someone deeply loved asks you to take in the utter finality of death. Death is the end of all possibility for your relationship to be any way other than it was, or to have more of what was good. The end of the opportunity to love is a lot to surrender to. Underlying the struggle against acceptance is probably a visceral longing to simply undo reality—to go back in time, to have another chance to get things right. The deepest wish is that most impossible of things: *to bring the person back to life.* Sometimes these desires, never to be fulfilled, will be held below the level of conscious awareness, because you are (unconsciously) aware of wanting what you know you cannot have. Yet if you can bring your longing (however unrealistic it may be) into the light of awareness, allowing its presence, along with feelings of guilt, regret, anger, or relief that may accompany grief—if you're able to acknowledge the extent of what's being grieved—you are more likely to face what's there to be faced, in a way that will enable you to come to peace, and to move on with your life, without this person whom you so loved.

Be alert to the mind's attempt to generate consoling thoughts as a way to distance you from the pain. *She had a long, good life. Now his suffering has come to an end.* You may seek to take refuge in memories of better times, to retreat to a "spiritual" interpretation of what's occurred. There may be an effort to "keep your mind off of it," as if forcing a stiff upper lip will somehow diminish or blunt the severity of the loss. Instead, stay in *feeling* as much as you can. Anything the mind wants to do is probably meant to hold the pain at bay. You're much better off letting yourself feel what's real.

The way to bring grieving to an end is to grieve.

Accepting Something in the Distant Past

In becoming more attuned to acceptance and resistance, you may turn to examine things in your past—in particular, painful history with a lasting impact, something unresolved or buried. You may see that you've been unable to accept a long-ago occurrence, something that happened to you or something you did (or neglected to do). Acceptance didn't feel possible at the time, especially if you were very young. The natural defense against pain led you to turn away.

You may think you're done with that painful history, and perhaps you are. Maybe it no longer haunts you; you don't identify with it anymore. There's no point in dredging up every issue from your past, in reopening an old wound, if you're truly done with a thing. If you aren't carrying an emotional remnant with you as you move through your days now, then let it be.

It may seem that time has relieved you of the pain of the harm or guilt. You may have convinced yourself that you're healed, because you "ought" to be, or because you've "risen above it," perhaps via a spiritual idea about detachment, telling yourself that the one with the painful past "isn't who you really are."

But if the memory still has the power to flood you with emotion, or if the long-term impact of what occurred continues to show up in how you live now, you owe it to yourself to reconsider the question of whether you're really done with the difficult history. If you identify with a piece of your past, you'd do well to revisit it—not in your mind, but in your heart and body.

Maybe you've learned to cope with the residue of the past via strategies to help you avoid "going there." You have a vocabulary or a story to account for what happened, something that protects you against what (still) hurts. Maybe you long ago despaired of ever fully letting it go. You believe that since nothing can change the fact that the thing took place, there's nothing to be done about the persisting pain.

Whatever you may tell yourself, if you still hurt when the memory visits you, then what took place is still, in some sense, part of your *present* reality. The long-ago inability to accept means you still carry a complex body of feelings about the past. Occasionally, they come near enough to the surface to cause you to suffer anew, almost as though the experience was still taking place.

The continuing pain asks you to pay attention, to see if you might come to an acceptance that wasn't possible historically, so that what took place can finally be where it belongs: in the past.

What's necessary is to acknowledge two truths:

(1) It really did happen.

(2) It's not happening anymore.

The persistent inability to accept that it happened is what keeps it (in effect) happening now.

Seeing the difference between the occurrence (in the past) and the resistance (still present) can itself be relieving. You cannot undo what happened. But you do have some say in how it affects you *now*. It's possible to accept now something that took place long ago. The way to do that is to surrender, without resistance, to the feelings that are stirred in present-day awareness.

Allow the fullness of rage, shame, fear, sorrow. If tears come, allow them. Whatever has been buried, surrender to it. Do not fear your feelings. (If you are concerned about this, don't hesitate to seek the support of a mental health professional.) If you find you're revisiting, in your mind's eye, particular scenes or moments from the past, allow yourself to go there, if you sense that doing so will enable you to feel what needs to be felt. You will very likely experience relief, if you give yourself to what you've avoided. Do not resort to the familiar refuge of the mind's attempt to minimize discomfort via storytelling or denial.

Remember, accepting the reality of what happened *is not approval*. In the case of something traumatic, it can seem like an offense to self to say *yes, this really happened*. Almost as if you were saying *it's okay* it happened. Acceptance is simply acknowledging the reality of a thing.

This is the way to really—finally—be done with it.

What About Hope?

How does accepting what-is relate to hope for the future? Hope is generally looked upon as a good thing. Its absence is thought to be indicative of despair. But what if neither of those is inevitably true? Hope can be looked at from a fresh perspective. Hope (like dread) is an expression of the familiar self. The self that you deeply are cannot be adversely affected (or benefited) by whatever is to come. So you can be sure that if you're engaged in hoping, you are indulging the invented self—which is the same self that's able to suffer when things don't turn out well . . . or to feel gratified or relieved when they do.

Why do we hope? Hope for a better future is often a way to endure unwelcome circumstances, or to get through a time of uncertainty, a situation where there's limited control of the outcome. In that time of waiting to see what will develop, hope can feel like "something to do," almost as if it might influence how things go. It creates a feeling of buoyancy, something that carries a person along in the getting from here to there.

The reality is that in the interval between the start of hope and when the outcome occurs, you *don't know* what's going to happen. The ego-mind dislikes not knowing. Feeling hope is a way of avoiding the discomfort of uncertainty.

Yet allowing the truth of not-knowing is a setup for peacefulness. Because you're accepting what-is: that you don't know and that you're not in control. If the in-between passage of time isn't colored by repeatedly wondering how things might turn out, or by envisioning how you'd like them to (or fear they might), you're much more likely to experience each intervening moment as it comes along. You won't be constantly robbed of presence by being in your head, spinning scenarios of the imagined future.

If you look at how hope functions—why it starts up, and where it focuses attention—you'll see that it puts you at a remove from presence. It looks to a desired future, not to this moment. You don't see the *now* because you're looking toward what might happen later. Since the future is accessible only via thinking, when you hope, you experience yourself not as presence but as a maker of thoughts.

Hope lays the groundwork for resistance. Declining to ask hope to carry you along increases the likelihood that when the outcome occurs, you'll acknowledge it with equanimity, whether or not it's what you wished for. If you look at the situations in which you experience resistance, they were often preceded by hope for some other reality, or by a background expectation that things would turn out a certain way. If each moment were allowed to be itself, without being compared with how you thought or hoped it would be, acceptance would occur much more readily. But because we move through our lives in a default stance of hoping things will develop in alignment with our preferences, we're constantly setting ourselves up for a challenge to natural acceptance.

If you've put your house on the market, the desired outcome clearly is that you'll get a buyer and that the house will sell for roughly the price you're asking. This situation contains multiple uncertainties, including the timing of the end point. There's no telling when (or if) the house will sell, or for how much. A lot may be riding on a possible sale (the prospect of buying a new house, taking on a new job). Anxiety over the unpredictable can morph into an uneasy hope. Intensifying hope can be like pouring gas on a fire. You have to work that much harder to hide from reality, since deeply you know the truth: that you have only so much to say in the matter of when/whether the house sells, and for how much. When the stakes are high, uncertainty is a difficult truth to allow.

Nevertheless, accepting the truth that you're not in control is the only possible way for you to move peacefully from here to there—from the day the realtor hammers the sign into your lawn to the day she calls with a closing date. *You don't know how it's going to turn out.* And hoping it goes the way you want will only rob you of all the days in between, because you will be living not in them, but in the desired (or dreaded) future.

It's entirely possible to have a preference without living in a sustained state of hopefulness. Of course you know what your preference is. Declining to let your life be run by hope does not ask indifference of you.

Isn't it necessary to hope to bring about positive things? Doesn't hope inspire good works in your life and in the larger world? The mind's ability to envision better things can give rise to creative ideas, opening the door to new possibility. Yet worthwhile action can be taken toward a desired end without attachment to outcome being the necessary fuel of each step along the way. Each part is done for its own sake, with focus and presence, even as there's the background awareness of the larger goal. Anything done with full attention (even when it's part of a larger whole) will be accomplished as well as it can be, increasing the likelihood of overall success.

What about hope that's generalized—the hope that you'll be happy someday, that one day the world will be without war? If hope is able to ripen into something you can do *now* to bring about the wished-for condition, then summon the will to take action toward that end. Otherwise, it's (only) a thought.

Most hope looks over the head of the now. It's often turned to as a way to avoid allowing some present disappointment or worry, a feeling that's alive in the moment. Rather than trying to avoid the present via dreams of a possible future, better to direct your attention *here.*

When Surrender Becomes the Default

As you come to experience how resistance only makes things worse, there will be times when you sense a tightening, the mind doing its muttering, but then awareness will dawn, and you'll ease into acceptance. The discomfort will subside, surrender taking the place of negativity. The *fact* of reality has assumed primacy over your *feeling* about it. You may watch yourself experience this a thousand times: you push against something, realize you're resisting, then soften. Countless episodes of it: tighten, notice, soften; tighten, notice, soften. You may suppose it will always be this way, that nonacceptance will remain the default. That you'll always have to "catch yourself," reminding yourself to yield.

But you may be in for a delicious surprise. Habits can unlearn themselves. The more you see how resistance causes suffering, the more likely it is that acceptance will become the automatic response. You don't have to remember not to resist, because it no longer occurs to you to do so. The whole question of whether or not you like something is less compelling than it used to be.

A thing takes place, and it simply *is*. You are softer than you used to be, not so easily thrown off-balance by life.

Even the most subtle degree of resistance keeps the familiar self enlivened. Yielding to what-is opens the door to experiencing your deep nature as a free being.

11

Living in Feeling: The Encounter with Reality

We are physical beings. Whatever a given moment may hold, the engagement with the present happens from within a body. The awareness of the immediate scene will vacillate, depending on what the mind's doing. But life is here and now, where the body is. When attention is even subtly on present reality, the senses are enlivened. Something is seen, heard, smelled, tasted, felt. The body's inner physicality, too, is experienced directly. The senses keep us attuned to ourselves: we feel tired, satiated, excited, tense. The body is its own private "environment," one that goes with us everywhere we go.

The Primary Response to Reality

Because we are animals, the primary encounter with our world is bodied. In infancy, the vehicle of encounter is the body. The profound satisfaction of physical comfort (relief from hunger, exertion, pain; the pleasure of tender or intimate touch) has no equal in human experience. The longing for bodily satisfaction stays with us all our lives, regardless of how much of life is spent in the head.

We *feel*—one another, ourselves, the world around us. The visceral experience of aliveness happens via feeling. Feeling shows up not only in response to something external. It's also generated within, experienced as the spontaneous will to do something. A feeling is what's behind many an impulse to move, to act. Feeling thirsty ripens into getting water to drink. Restlessness stirs the idea of going for a walk. A loving feeling leads to the desire for attentiveness or intimacy.

While the primary experience of feeling relates to physical sensation (the body in motion, in contact with something), the word *feel* has come to encompass any inner response resulting from an encounter with reality, whether or not it's physical in nature. When something "touches" a person, it's "felt" inside. We even use *feel* as a synonym for "think" or "believe": the mind in contact with reality "feels" one thing or another about it.

Even with our highly evolved brains (able to create entirely non-physical "realities"), even as we insert our ceaselessly busy minds into practically every bodied encounter with life, the original *feeling* response is still very much alive, moment to moment. But feeling happens so spontaneously, so quickly, and is registered at such a deep level that it often escapes conscious noticing. This primary response isn't seen because of how swiftly and liquidly the mind gets involved, co-opting that initial, instantaneous moment of feeling.

The Secondary Response to Reality

The mind moves with lightning speed, especially when that initial response was something you'd just as soon not linger over. The *mental* processing of what's happening is likely to generate a reactive *emotion*, a second-generation "feeling" that may bear little resemblance to the original, authentic, deeply felt response.

That thought-driven emotion has an agenda: to protect you from the original feeling that you don't want to stay with.

You're driving your car along the highway when you glance in your rear view mirror to see that a tractor-trailer has pulled up close behind you, practically riding your bumper. You're both going nearly eighty. Traffic is heavy; it would be hard to change lanes. If you suddenly had to hit the brakes, there'd be no way the truck could avoid slamming into you.

You'd like to give the driver a piece of your mind. As you try to maintain your speed, occasionally looking back and seeing he still hasn't backed off, you feel your blood start to boil.

By the time the anger is ripening, a lot has already happened, though you're not likely to have paid attention to the preceding stages. At the first sight of the truck's grille filling your mirror, there was instantaneous, visceral fear. The very earliest response was felt in the body—the heart starting to pound, the hands tightly gripping the steering wheel—*not* in the mind. The next instant, though, the mind started up, playing movies of the accident that could happen, spinning a narrative about the idiot driver, about how *he thinks because he has a big rig he rules the road.*

What's happened is that the mental activity took hold of the animal terror of death and distorted it into anger. All of this happened in a split second. As far as you'd probably be able (or willing) to report, what took place inside you, in response to the truck pulling up close behind you, was simply fury. Getting angry at the driver helps you feel some control—which was nowhere to be found when you first looked in the mirror, with its urgent message of danger.

We do this all the time.

Say you've been seeing a woman for a few months. You really enjoy one another. You share many common interests, laugh a lot, have great times in bed. In the three years since your twenty-year marriage ended, it's the first time you've come to really care for someone. You've even been thinking of broaching the subject of living together. At her apartment one afternoon, you're about to bring up the idea when she announces she doesn't want to see you anymore. You're stunned. Hurt. You thought she cared for you as much as you care for her.

On the desolate drive back to your house, you begin thinking. *I'm better off being alone. Life's simpler that way.* By the time you pull into your driveway, you've decided she wasn't so great anyhow, not all that easy to get along with.

Inside the house, you kick off your shoes and pull a beer out of the fridge. Mutter something about how women aren't worth all the trouble. She always did remind you of your ex-wife, kind of edgy and manipulative like that. Pretty soon what so recently were tender feelings have morphed into contempt. You're relieved to be done with her.

Anything to avoid feeling hurt and confused.

Sometimes, it's anything to avoid getting your hopes up, or lingering over something that just plain feels good (as if you might spook your good fortune into abandoning you). One morning your boss tells you you're doing a great job. Instead of just savoring the moment of deep satisfaction, which was the primary feeling, you start thinking, *God, I hope I don't screw up.* The next thing you know, you've gone from feeling appreciated to feeling worried, revisiting how things deteriorated on your last job, where that boss initially thought you were terrific. The worry has caused you to completely lose touch with that original feeling of gratification.

Say a stranger smiles at you, where the two of you are standing on a busy corner, waiting for the light to change. There's a penetrating expression in those blue eyes, on that lovely face . . . and for a moment, you are enjoying seeing and being seen, simply that. But then the mind horns in. *Maybe that's bemusement in those eyes, because broccoli's stuck between my teeth.*

We almost can't stand to just feel what's here, whether it's delicious or uncomfortable. But what if we could? Just for the few moments that the feeling's alive, fresh, original—what if we could feel the aliveness of just being with it?

The Experience of a Moment

What happens, in a given moment of life? Something is taking place, and according to the degree to which it seems to be about you, there's probably some kind of inner response. This phenomenon is ongoing. Even something that doesn't involve bodily contact is experienced on the level of feeling.

The feeling response is deep in, private, spontaneous. It's nothing you can control or see coming; it just *happens*. The encounter of awareness with the present is the experience of aliveness. A moment truly lived is a *felt* moment. Present with what's happening, you experience something inside. This response (which may include sensory impressions) is the earliest indication of having been affected by something. It precedes thought, or any kind of emotional or behavioral reaction. That felt response is what gets thinking to start up in the first place, with emotion quickly following.

Whether you are more emotional or mental in your orientation to reality, the original impression comes as feeling. People who say they are cerebral are no less affected, in that very earliest moment of response, than those who consider themselves primarily emotional. Each initially feels something; each typically takes refuge in thought as a way to avoid staying with the feeling.

But there *is* a difference between the two types of people. At the point where the mind kicks in, the more "in-the-head" person will attempt to *stay* in thought, using it to avoid or manage the prior feeling. This person will aspire (seldom successfully) to keep thought from generating a reactive emotional response. The primary strategy for this person is to process, understand, and evaluate what's happened, with the goal of moderating or avoiding emotions. For the more emotion-based person, the thought (used to protect against the uncomfortable initial feeling) will readily set in motion a complex of reactive emotions, which (unresisted) are allowed to take on a momentum of their own.

The emotionally reactive state is twice removed from the authentic, original *feeling* response. Yet the two are often confused, mistaken for a single thing. The primary, spontaneous feeling is often lost, buried, subsumed by the secondary emotional uproar.

Both types of people have lost track of the primary response—the one that has to do with presence. The apparent difference between cerebral and heartfelt is minor. What's significant is their common avoidance of the primary feeling.

Once an emotional reaction has taken on a life of its own, more and more thoughts are generated to support, defend, and justify the developing ruckus. *I hope some cop gets that truck driver before he kills somebody.* By this time, any possible awareness of the original feeling is lost in the noise and commotion. *Come to think of it, my girlfriend never was the one to initiate a date or sex. How could I have been so blind as to think she cared for me?*

Caught up in the storm of mental/emotional activity you've brewed, you're hardly able to show up for whatever comes next, as life continues its ceaseless unfolding. Your awareness is entirely focused on what you cannot let go of, the residue of a life experience that has already come and gone. You are living in the past. The present is passing you by.

How Does Feeling Relate to Suffering?

You may have been supposing that reducing suffering has everything to do with steering *away* from feelings, especially the difficult ones. Or that the key to suffering less is to *manage* the feeling state: to focus on upbeat, positive feelings and not linger in the painful ones.

Maybe you've been imagining that if you wake up, you won't *feel* things anymore.

Chances are, these beliefs are there because you're confusing the authentic feeling response with the emotions subsequently generated by thought. The spontaneous primary response must be distinguished from the whirlwind of emotion set in motion by reactive thinking. "Being in touch with your feelings" is often touted as a good thing, a way to "be in your heart," to live a life that balances the thinking part of you with the feeling part. Yet this approach typically neglects the distinction between an original deeply felt response and the thought-driven emotion that comes in its wake, that becomes its own (often painful) egoic reality. If you want to discover ways to suffer less, learn to distinguish one from the other. The two are worlds apart. The mind-generated one is where suffering is forged. The other—authentic feeling—is where life is actually lived. It's where presence senses itself.

Never mind any question of whether the spontaneous feeling response might be egoic in nature—that is, whether its source is the conditioned, identified self. What's significant, in terms of consciousness, is that it occurs spontaneously, in the lived moment. It's *real*. It's here, alive, part of the moment (prior to the mind getting hold of it, creating distance from the present). Even if you think you can see the feeling's origin in conditioning, that understanding comes *after the fact*—and is therefore secondary. The point is to live in the *primary:* the feeling response.

After awakening, life continues to give rise to feelings. Being awake doesn't mean you stop feeling. If you walk outside into a blowing snowstorm, you will very likely experience a surge of excitement. If you watch a child figuring out how to tie her shoelace, you'll feel a warm flood of delight. Visualizing the suffering in the aftermath of a tsunami, you will almost certainly be filled with sorrow. In the awake state, life is lived largely in moment-to-moment feeling. Each thing is felt, allowed, and allowed to pass.

It's neither good nor bad to feel. It's simply a fact of life, a function of being alive in the world, in a body. The immediate response to a moment of life is as real as whatever's happening outside of yourself.

The question is, how aware are you of it, when it comes? How willing are you to feel—to allow—that primary response?

Feeling as the Door to Presence

When you allow yourself to feel, to live your own real response to what's happening, you're present. When you linger there, declining to take that next, oh-so-familiar step of resorting to thinking as a coping measure (*doing something* with the primary response), you're better able to yield to accept whatever is happening. The result is that you're less likely to outwardly react in a way you might later wish you hadn't. You may be able to watch some story try to start up, and experience quite vividly the living option to decline to indulge it.

Moreover, how you deal with this moment has everything to do with whether it will burden you afterward. Staying with that original sensation means you're less likely to carry forward, into subsequent moments, any emotional residue from the experience. You may be relieved of the lifelong tendency for something to cling, in the aftermath of experience, like lint or a bad smell—for it to continue to affect you long after the moment has passed. When you allow a feeling its due, then you're able to move on from it.

You don't have to *do* anything with the feeling (account for it, label it, make up a story about it, project ahead to what's next). Just feel it. Felt, allowed, it will likely dissolve—often about as quickly as the moment that generated it gives way to the next one. You're able to move on, to enter the next moment freshly—to feel *it*.

A feeling that's fully allowed often will not result in any thought at all. Since the mind is where the seeds of suffering are sown, a moment that's felt, not mentally processed, is a moment that doesn't give rise to suffering—*even if it's a moment that's difficult.*

Much of the emotional burden you now carry began life as a pushed-away feeling. There was a spontaneous felt response to some life development, but then it was mentally managed and distorted into an emotional mess, which you've never managed to put down, and which now interferes with your ability to encounter newly arriving reality.

The idea is to not have to let go, later, of what has become a burden, but rather *to not hold on in the first place.* Not holding on doesn't mean being at a forced distance from what's happening, but being fully *with* it.

Suffering is generated by what you do in the presence of reality. It isn't caused by being present with what you actually feel, in response to something that's happening right now. It's brewed the moment the mind decides it's got to do something with a feeling.

Don't be afraid of feelings, even uncomfortable ones. Allowing them is how you sense yourself in the present moment. It puts you directly in touch with reality: your own. Spontaneous feeling is as much a part of the moment's reality as what's taking place outwardly. Being attuned to reality is the door to presence—to experiencing yourself not as a reactive, limited ego-mind, but rather as pulsing, alive awareness.

When you live such that your moment-to-moment encounter with reality is rooted in feeling, your inner state is constantly new, fresh, in flux. Because outer reality is constantly in flux. It's not a static thing, ever.

Whatever is happening, feel it. Live *there.*

12

Fear

The phenomenon of fear is surely one of the most impressive proofs of the mind's power to convince us of the reality of its contents. For most of the things that stir fear arrive in the form of thoughts. All-consuming dread, inner films of nightmares running on a ceaseless loop, sleepless nights—these things are set in motion by the mind, whose content is usually at a remove from present reality. Even if a thought is of some factual threat (out there somewhere, some-when), the vast majority of the time, the threat that's brewing the fear is not immediate. The direct cause of the present distress is not danger itself, but a mental picture of danger.

But the body and the psyche don't readily distinguish literal physical danger from a mind-made image of it, with resulting terrible cost to one's physical and emotional well-being. Such is the power of the human mind. What the mind says is real, the body and emotions treat as real. Adrenalin flows (but uselessly). The muscles tense (but there is nothing to run from). The body is on high alert, the heart racing, the breath quick (but there's no actual predator; instead, you just cannot sleep).

If a person could reduce all possible episodes of fear down to those threats that are imminent, life would be very much less a scary place.

Then again, as we will see, even danger that's material and immediate doesn't inevitably elicit a fear response. In a situation of true danger, there often isn't time to be afraid. There is time only to act.

Fear, largely, is a waste of good life, one of the most capable thieves of presence. Not to mention love.

What Causes Fear

Fear is nature's way of calling attention to a threat, so you can do something to prevent harm—to stop what's happening, minimize the damage, escape. When the threat is real and immediate, fear has a useful function. It gets the juices flowing, gets you moving, makes you resourceful, capable. Fear is an appropriate, possibly beneficial response when a train is coming down the track your car is stalled on, or when a rabid dog has you cornered in an alleyway.

But fear that comes from thinking—which is to say, summoning to awareness a thing that's *not* here-and-now—does not serve you at all. It actually *causes* harm—to your equanimity, and perhaps to your physical well-being. Mind-caused fear has the power to rob you of life, because it replaces whatever the present moment might have been with gripping anxiety and an unending stream of distressing thoughts and images. Most fear is pointless—and preventable.

Sometimes fear is fueled by a real situation, a life development fraught with the potential for instability, loss, or danger. Such things as life-threatening illness or financial jeopardy can introduce a steady drip of worry into a person's life. Yet even in an ongoing situation like that, most particular moments will *not* carry imminent threat. They will be—if they can be allowed to be—simply *life.*

Most episodes of fear are set in motion by one of these things: the prospect of some future development (predictable or imagined), the vast unknowable (that is, life's general unpredictability), or the feeling of not being in control. None of these is a present threat to well-being. The primary cause of fear is *not* the imminent threat of a known negative force. It's a thought about a possible or shapeless future.

The dynamic behind fear needs to be brought into the light of awareness, revealing the common assumptions that put a person at its mercy. The same mind whose activity breeds crippling worry can be used to disable the torture machine. When you understand the role the mind plays in generating fear, you can apply that same intelligence to achieving a more peaceful encounter with actual (or imagined) challenges. In this effort to reduce suffering, the mind can become an ally.

Bad Things *Will* Happen (and Nobody's Getting Out of Here Alive)

Challenge and loss are inevitable in every life, your own and the lives of those you care about. Only some of the hard things that come down the pike will be readily manageable or avoidable. Death, for instance, *will* not be sidestepped (your own or others').

One of the assumptions driving fear is this:

Since bad things are inevitable, fear must be inevitable.

Do you think an awake person is unaware that bad things will happen? No one is exempt from life. Yet it's possible to live without fear, and not because of cluelessness or aloofness.

How does a person stand in clear-eyed recognition of inevitable challenge and loss *and yet not be driven by anxiety and fear*? With the ongoing awareness that much of life is beyond a person's control and that life is full of unpredicted things, how is it possible to live with equanimity?

But it is. And you don't have to wait for full awakeness to do it.

Not One Thing, but Two

A good start to dismantling fear is to look at another assumption, one you've probably made all your life:

The cause of fear is the feared thing itself.

We're at the mercy of fear because we think fear is caused by scary things. Since danger, decay, and uncertainty are known to be inevitable, then (the logic goes) it's not possible to be without fear.

As long as you believe this to be true, it will seem as though the only way to get fear to subside is to triumph over the thing "causing" the fear—to solve or escape the problem. Understanding that the feared thing is not the direct cause of fear asks you first to see as separate things what you've probably seen as one: the frightening thing and the fear it elicits. When you see that they're not inextricably tied, it becomes possible to address each in turn, to give each its due attention. Treating them as separate phenomena opens the door to peacefulness, *even in the presence of a possible danger or challenge.* We will look at ways to address each one.

The actual cause of fear is the stream of thoughts generated in the presence of the mind's image of what could befall you or someone you care for. Identifying the source of fear as mental activity won't immediately dissolve the fear. It *will* draw some attention from the feared thing, directing it to the workings of your mind. As you discover the power of thoughts to transform a possible future danger into an apparently real and present threat, ease will enter the picture, and you won't be so at the mercy of fear.

The Insanity of Fear

Chances are, if you're *aware* of feeling fearful, it's not in response to an actual, immediate threat. It's in response to something you're thinking about. If you're feeling afraid, it's likely there's nothing to be afraid of, *in this moment.*

What a radical proposition this is. It surely flies in the face of what you've supposed. Fear generally appears unavoidable (that is, justified), because it's so all-consuming, and because often, if you look around, you *can* point to something "real" that seems to have caused it.

But what if it were true that most fear is unnecessary? What if most episodes of fear could be dismantled, or fail to start up at all? What would that feel like? How wonderful to have fear be a rare visitor! To have it take hold only at those times when it has a useful function—when it might actually protect you or another.

If you can come to see that most fear is in response to a thought, you'll have taken a significant step toward equanimity. If you neglect looking at the anatomy of your own episodes of fear, you'll continue being at its mercy.

Key to understanding the anatomy of fear is this:

All that will ever be real is now.

Again and again, this truth has the power to set you free. Life is the present. The mind will insist that life is *also* what thought can anticipate or recall. But thought, even "true" thought, is not life itself. It will always be at a remove, because it's an abstracted representation of life. When you're deep in projection, you're missing the *now.* Thought distracts you from life.

How many times must you look at this before it takes you over completely? The present is what's real. Everything else is in the head.

What's here, present, immediate?

If what's real now is physical pain, you surrender to it, doing what you can to ameliorate the discomfort. There's no spare energy for fearing future painful moments. If you project ahead, see that the mind is doing that. The fear is directed at a thought, whose content is pain-not-yet-here.

If you've learned you have a disease that will eventually cause severe pain, what's real *now* is that you're taking in this difficult information about your health. Pain is not in the picture of present reality. If you feel afraid, see that your fear is caused by a thought, not by reality. Each part of the predictable illness will unfold in *some* present time, but it's not here *now*. Regarding thoughts about something reasonably predictable, the mind wants to protest, *But they might be* true *thoughts!* This is not about whether the thoughts are true. It's about whether in *this moment* there is actual harm coming to you. It's about learning to distinguish potential future threat from actual present danger.

Say you're in the woods and have just walked around a bend, startling a mother bear and her cub. At the sight of the mother's aggressive stance, your heart will certainly pound. Clearly, this is a fear that's appropriate, that serves you. Quickly, though, the fear will give way to practical physical response. No time to linger in fear. Your primary experience (the new *now*) will doubtless be the motion of getting out of there. A physical experience, not a mental one. If you could somehow pause in the middle of this true emergency and make note of your interior, you'd probably see not fear so much as extreme and focused physical exertion. In such a situation of extremity, nature has built us (animals, after all) such that all resources are brought to avoiding harm with an economy of effort. Once the fact of the danger is processed, the mind is of little use, kicking in only when it's needed to figure out, on the spot, what to do: which way to run.

What the essential peaceful self longs to rest in, always, is reality. In the presence of the real, there is peace. The future can never be real, because only the present ever exists. Deeply, this is known. Asking yourself to believe the mind when it insists on the reality of its thoughts, its vivid imagery, is inviting yourself to be crazy.

Is something about the *now* threatening your well-being? How much of your inner state has to do with thinking itself?

If the threat of something difficult is looming, and you have good reason to believe it will come about, there are likely to be thoughts insisting that the severity and/or the predictability of the imagined future mean that it's, in some sense, already real. But see the difference between present reality and *thoughts* about one that appears predictable.

Something in a person wants to believe that if fear is strong enough, it will somehow offer protection against the possible terrible things out there. Something wants to suppose that it's possible to brace yourself for a prospective difficulty, as if being afraid in advance will make it easier to cope when the time comes. You may tell yourself you're trying to accept what *might* happen, wanting to believe that ahead-of-time acceptance somehow justifies the future-directed thoughts. But since it isn't possible to accept what isn't real (that is, present), all you're doing is inducing pointless suffering *now*. However much you may wish to believe that anticipating something difficult will prepare you for it by (in effect) getting the suffering going ahead of time, you'll *still* have to face the actual development, if the dreaded thing actually materializes (which, as you may have noticed, isn't always how it goes).

Living in the future means you live the dreaded thing *twice*— or, more likely, hundreds of times: the one time it actually takes place, and the myriad times you've played it in your head in advance. If you count all the times you've worried about something that never even came to pass, when you take the measure of all the useless worry, the amount of suffering you might have been spared can bring tears to your eyes.

Feeling afraid is completely crazy. It does nothing but cause suffering. When there's no immediate threat, fear saves you from nothing.

Amorphous Fear

Sometimes fear has no obvious or particular cause. There's an undercurrent of generalized anxiety in the presence of life's perennial uncertainty and chaos, a voice inside murmuring that any minute all hell could break loose. Keeping on top of news developments, for some, can generate a steady current of dread aimed at things beyond anyone's control or understanding: meteorological or environmental disasters, terrorist attacks, a severe economic downturn, a drunk driver.

A lot of what fuels fear is the background awareness that we don't know what's going to come and are largely at the mercy of forces beyond our control. If you ever doubt the truth of life's radical unpredictability, all you have to do is look back ten years and ask, *Could I have dreamed then where I'd be now, what would have befallen me and those I love?*

When virtually everything about the future is unknowable, the mind fills in the vacuum by spinning scenarios of the possible. Imagining awful developments can seem somehow preferable to simply allowing as how you aren't in control, and you don't know how things are going to turn out. But if it's being with the truth that brings peace, then the thing to do is to try to relax in the face of *don't-know* and *can't-control*. Staying with the plain truth of the situation, even when it leaves you with a lot of unanswerable questions, can bring you to peacefulness. It can help your mind to take a rest from scenario-spinning, leaving you to just be in the moment. *This* one—which is likely not full of danger. That's all you have to do. It's all you *can* do.

When you attempt to grasp onto an illusion of predictability, when you try to manage unwieldy forces not within your control, you're set up for anxiety, continual frustration, and being thrown off-balance by the unexpected. If you can get your sea legs, taking each roll of the vessel as it comes, it's much more possible to relax into the view of the ever-changing scenery.

If you're waiting for everything to settle down, for every possible negative thing to be magically taken care of, you're not inhabiting the real world. Living contentedly is learning to live in comfortable recognition of the truth that things are ceaselessly uncertain. The sooner you can make your peace with this, the more you'll be able to savor your moments of life—the vast majority of which are ordinary, plainly miraculous, and absent threat of any kind.

When Fear Has Hold of You

There's no mistaking the consuming presence of fear. Because it feels so bad, it calls attention to itself. Still, because the mind is so good at convincing you of the reality of its thoughts, and because fear seems inherent to the feared thing, in a fearful time, the primary attention is not on the emotion itself but on the scary situation.

Any moment you become self-aware is an opening. Move your attention from the *thoughts* about the feared thing to how you're *feeling* about it. Look around at the inner landscape. Without drifting back toward thoughts of the dreaded future, be with the physical sensation of fear. Feel how it hurts, how consuming it is of attention, of presence. See how fear makes it virtually impossible to experience anything else.

Just see this. Don't attempt to change anything.

Now, redirect attention from the sensation of fear to the activity of your mind. Look at the thoughts and pictures that have been occupying your awareness. Notice that it's these stories—not the immediate scene—that have generated the fear. See if you can observe your mind *without* (just for now) getting reengaged in the compelling "reality" of the mental movie. Be alert to thoughts insisting that "this really *is* how it's likely to go." Even if that seems to be true, right now all you're doing is looking at the contents of your mind, without regard for their apparent validity.

The mind wants you to think that if "it's true" the projected nightmare is likely to become actualized in some future moment, somehow this *present-moment* fear is justified. Watch the mind insist upon this. Keep watching; don't get drawn back into its siren song. If you do get sucked back in, the next moment you become self-aware, begin again to look at the thoughts driving the fear.

You're moving back and forth between watching the movie in your head—being (as it were) in the audience—and being a participant in the drama. You're vacillating between seeing the feared thing *as drama* and believing it's reality. Notice yourself doing one or the other. See that you have the ability to observe the mental story as phenomenon, to *see* it rather than to occupy it. Even if only fleetingly.

Now, allow your attention to move to the immediate scene of this moment. Let the contents of your mind, as well as the sensation of fear, drift into the background of awareness. Just for a few moments, you can do this. Focus on the present-moment scene—this place, this momentary reality. Ask yourself, *What is here that's a threat?*

Remember, chances are very good that if you have the leisure to direct your attention to such a question, there *is* no immediate danger. Because if there were, you'd be busily responding (running from the bear), not wasting energy on fear-inducing thoughts.

Bringing awareness to physical reality, both the scene around you and your bodily sensations, can be a potent support to tuning into presence, a way to blessed relief from the suffering caused by the mind.

Learning to focus attention in this way, to shift it from one thing to the other, is the beginning of the liberating ability to address fear as one thing and the real-life challenge as another. To be able to take practical, possibly beneficial steps in the direction of improving the situation, while not being crippled by worry.

Addressing a Scary Situation

It's possible to face challenging circumstances without being constantly fearful. Here is where the clear-thinking mind can be a blessing in the work to reduce fear. Rather than allowing the mind to spin terrible possible outcomes or escape from the difficult situation, instead direct it toward reality, working in sync with it. Looking at the circumstances that life has visited upon you, see if you can delineate each of the following:

- The *immediate* difficulty versus what's likely or possible *later*
- What's *known* versus what's *not known*
- What you might *do something* about versus what's *beyond your control*
- What needs *doing now* versus what will need to be *done later*

You may find it helpful to make lists, or simply to write out your thoughts as they come. Perhaps you'll discuss your findings with a friend or some other supportive person. (It might be preferable to not enlist the support of someone affected by the same situation, although if both of you are able to keep to the task, it may be helpful to both.) Throughout this process, take great care to separate what's *presently* real from what could/will come later.

Anytime you notice yourself supposing that the only way the fear will stop is if things turn out okay, remind yourself that the situation and the fear are *distinct things,* and must be treated separately. The outcome of the effort to minimize fear depends upon addressing these as separate issues.

Once you've gotten clear about the parameters of your situation, as it's presently understood, you can get down to living with its realities, in a way that won't have you in a constant state of worry and anxiety.

Especially with a situation that's overwhelming, long-term, or loaded with uncertainty, it's crucial to focus attention only on what's real *now.* Address what currently needs addressing. You may find there's actually *nothing* presently compelling action, and you can rest from any concern at all. Anytime you notice yourself looking ahead to what could possibly happen next, or eventually, realize that you've slipped into the world of thought, and gently return your attention to the present.

At any particular moment of looking at your situation, some things will be known and others will not. Keep clear about the difference, so you can deal appropriately with each. Known facts about the situation must be accepted, however painful or life-altering they may be, if you want to keep from intensifying the pain of a difficult situation by adding resistance. Though it's often done with the mistaken impression it will protect you, resistance only compounds suffering and fuels the engine of fear. Feel whatever feelings come with surrendering to the truth. You may be surprised to find that you actually experience relief simply by accepting the hard realities. Even if the situation is objectively bleak, there's something peace-inducing (and fear-reducing) about relaxing into the truth. When you accept what can only be accepted, then it becomes possible to move forward to necessary or desirable action.

The gaping hole of the *unknown* must also be seen for what it is. Since the mind dislikes not-knowing, when it's confronted with uncertainty, it will tend to invent *some* story about the possible, and that invention (as we have seen) can create its own impression of reality, with the result of more fear, not less. Accepting the reality that there are unanswerable questions can give the mind the permission it needs to rest from agonizing scenario-spinning. A lot of unnecessary fear comes of avoiding the blunt fact of uncertainty. Instead of recoiling from these difficult truths, turn *toward* them, acknowledging the inherent limits on what's within your grasp. Being with the truth is a recipe for peace, even if the truth (here, uncertainty) is unwelcome.

Separate what you might influence from what you cannot. Take a slow, deep bow to the truth that other forces than you are at work here. Able to rest from suffering over what's not in your control, you're able to do what *can* be done without becoming uselessly distracted by if-onlys and what-ifs.

Sorting out what can be done *now* from what might be done *later* enables you to focus valuable resources where they will have an effect. Rest from needless and repetitive anticipation and planning. In a complex or novel life development, some planning may be advised. But do only what's necessary *now*. When the time comes for each thing, you'll focus on it then. Probably you can use all the rest you can get.

With each of these elements of a frightening situation, the key to facing the challenge, without being crippled by fear, is to fully be with what is true.

Imagine your way into the following experience.

You got laid off today, totally without warning. The job wasn't the perfect match for your skills and interests, but it did pay the bills. The initial shock quickly gave way to anger, which lasted through the evening. But now you're in bed, mulling a bleak situation: the prospect of only one more paycheck, your meager savings, and the paltry unemployment you'll be getting. Your mind is starting to play movies of how bad things might get in the coming weeks and months.

Then you see: the absence of a job and the money shortage will do nothing bad to you tonight. Right now, as you're lying here, everything is the same as it was. The walls are still standing around your bed. Your heart's continuing to beat. You still have the same smarts that got you that job you just lost.

What's known, now, is that you do not have a job. Another part of reality is the uncertainty about what's ahead. There simply is no way of knowing how long you'll be unemployed, or how much money you'll make if and when you get a new job, or whether your bills will get behind.

You take a big, deep breath in the presence of it all.

Tonight, in your pajamas, there's nothing you can do, apart from thinking of places you might look in the next few days. You've thought of several, but nothing else is coming to you just now.

You turn your attention to the quiet in the room, the sound of that one bird out in the dark trees somewhere. You feel how worn out your body is from the strain of the day, and how very good the bed feels. Sometimes your mind starts up again, imagining the prospect of losing your house because of getting behind in mortgage payments. But then you remember: *I'm in my bed, that's it. I'm in my pajamas, unemployed, and there's nothing to do right now but rest.*

You know that tomorrow, when you get up, you'll get busy scanning the job ads online, making sure you've got nice, clean clothes to interview in, figuring out ways to economize in the uncertain days ahead.

But now, the bed sure does feel good. And that bird out there is a reminder that the world is bigger than your lack of a job.

Fear of Death

Someday, you may be told you have only a few months to live. Maybe you've already been told this. You realize there may be pain or reduction of some kind, as you move toward the last day, the final moment.

Whether you're given advance notice or not, you know you will one day face your death. But now—*now, now*—you are alive. How can you possibly cope with the prospect of death, perhaps the likelihood of a radically shortened life, unless you feel your aliveness each moment? You are clearly not on your death bed. In fact, you notice that you feel quite fine. It doesn't mean you've forgotten what's ahead. It's just that *ahead* is—well, not now. Focusing on this present moment is a way to rest from what your mind wants to keep reminding you about the long-term picture.

The truth is, we only ever live in the moment. Sometimes it takes a life-threatening illness or severe financial difficulties to drive this home. Ask yourself, as many times as you need to, *What's real right now?*

Unless it's knocking on the door this very moment, is death real? The perfect definition of madness is to fear something that's both not here now and absolutely unavoidable. Are you planning not to die? The fact that death is inevitable makes fearing it a complete waste of pain.

The way we generally manage our knowledge of the certainty of death is to live as though it weren't so. We pretend, day to day, minute to minute, not to know this thing that we know. A lot is riding on this denial. Putting things off, for instance. Wasting life energy on things that don't matter. Thinking rather than living, which is to say, missing the present moment.

Then, when somebody dies unexpectedly, we are truly shocked. When our own death is suddenly revealed to be imminent, we can hardly believe it could be so. As if we thought it all might go on indefinitely.

Here's another case where living with reality is peace-inducing. What's real is that we know we will die and that we know the timing is uncertain. We constantly don't know whether life will still be going on this time next week, or even ten minutes from now.

What's it like to live with the frank, ongoing awareness that death could come (to self or other) at any time, to live without the underlying expectation of continuing? What's it like to exist in radical uncertainty and yet not be in a state of constant vigilance, anticipating doom at every turn?

See if you can find out. Apply what you've learned about fear to the prospect of your own death.

In a sense, every fear is a shadow of the big fear—the one that you will someday no longer exist.

This would be a good time to revisit the idea of what's meant by "you."

The reason fear can happen at all is that there's an underlying belief that something bad could happen to you. All fear flowers in the environment of the impression that you are your limited, ego-based self. Since this self is constructed and maintained within the walls of the mind, it's only natural that fear too would be created in the cramped, airless space of the self-referential ego-mind.

When you wake up, all fear, including the fear of physical death, goes away. This is because what "you" have turned out to be isn't something that's subject to harm.

When you wake up, in a sense you just died. The you that's always seemed so real and important—so worthy of protection, of feeling fear—has ceased to believe in itself. Associating physical death with the end of self is based on a mistaken idea. *Not* (as it may appear) because there's continuation beyond death, but because the narrowly defined self can "die" well in advance of the cessation of brain activity.

Nothing more wonderful could befall you.

13

The Creation and Care
of the Familiar Self

When you bring to mind a picture of yourself, inside and out,
what do you see? What are your defining features? What do you
enjoy? What do you believe is important? What are you good
at? What are you like physically speaking? When attention flows
from you, who or what does it move toward? What significant
things have happened in your life to make you into who you
are? What is your work in the world?

All of this makes you who you are, on the level of the familiar self. This person that you appear to be convinces you daily,
hourly, of its substance and importance. A lot of effort is devoted
to keeping this self happy and safe, and to maintaining the
impression that this is who you deeply are (even if you "know"
that isn't true). Lifelong attention is given to the effort to establish and uphold your identity, someone capable of doing good
things in the world and reaching personal fulfillment. Even if
you're a spiritual seeker, intent on being free of limiting identity,
this is almost certainly true of you. (Part of your identity may, in
fact, derive from being a seeker.)

The reality of the familiar self, as well as the perceived worthiness of the effort to keep it going, is something that mostly goes unexamined, in day-to-day life, for the very good reason that the alternative doesn't look very appealing. Contemplating a life without a well-defined self (even when that self includes things you'd just as soon do without) can conjure a life of despair, a meaningless existence, a negation of life. The main reason the idea of dying is so unwelcome, after all, is that it signifies the end of oneself. Death is difficult to conceive of—not perhaps the demise itself (the illness, the accident), so much as the radical *ceasing to be*. After all, as far back as you're able to remember, the world has had you in it.

The question is, who are you? Is the person you appear to be what you are at your essence?

Everyone assumes some kind of identity vis-à-vis other people. You are a particular someone in your present family, in your family of origin. You play certain roles in social and work settings. What you *do,* what you appear to *be* (successful, timid, defensive, youthful), naturally becomes part of your identity, both as you see yourself and as others see you (though there's often an unrecognized discrepancy between the two). It all becomes fastened onto "you," in the same tenacious way that what you think and feel about some life event gets fastened onto it.

But the roles you play, the features you exhibit, the things you believe in—while they matter very much in the ordinary realm of human discourse—are not what you *are*. When presence senses itself within you, none of these things have any substance. The more strongly you identify with these ultimately superficial features, the more you are certain to suffer.

Who Is it That Suffers?

Suffering takes place not because bad things happen, but because of the impression that this familiar self (the one bad things "happen to") is who you fundamentally *are*. Yet if you imagine ceasing to identify with all you define yourself as being, you probably have trouble imagining you could still *be*. So you naturally recoil from the prospect of letting it all go, hanging on to whatever you think of as being *you*.

The trouble is, that self cannot hope to sidestep all of life's periodic miseries. It will never be able to exert sufficient control over the ups and downs to put life on an even keel. This is why suffering is said to be inevitable. But it's inevitable *only if you identify with the self that's able to suffer.*

If you're looking at all of this because you wish to move through life with greater ease and well-being, the place to look is here: your sense of who you are, and how that is generated, and what sustains (and threatens) it.

If you want to suffer less but insist on trying to accomplish that by attempting to manage or avoid the outward apparent causes of suffering, you are walking up a mountain of sand. Probably, you're very tired by now, maybe more tired than you've realized.

If you really want to get somewhere, much better to just stand still and look around at where you are, not at where you want to get. Look inside to locate the source of your sense of self, the moorings and outline of that familiar person you seem to be. The one that identifies with a body of beliefs, the one that's a certain person privately and in the world, that's been shaped by its particular life experiences.

See what you can discover about how you maintain the self that's able to suffer.

It isn't necessary to try to stop identifying with your opinions, looks, work, significant life experiences; with the roles you play in relation to other people; with your gender, sexual orientation, social and economic status. What's needed is to see that you *do* identify with all of these things—to look with open eyes and a calm willingness to notice everything that constitutes your identity. To recognize it as *your identity,* and to learn to distinguish that from the presence of something real and alive in you that is *not* about any of those things. To see how when something good happens in your life, it gives the impression that it has to do with the really real you. To see how when a setback comes, the experience is that *you,* deep in, have been diminished.

Ceasing to identify comes about not by trying to stop the identification. But the detachment *can* come about—all on its own, as it were—simply by the willingness (gutsy, at times) to see how much you *do* identify. To recognize the meaning you derive from what you do and are, what you're good at, the things you believe to be true. (It's not about whether they're true, or important; it's about whether you allow them to define you.)

Is there anything about yourself that, if it were lost or put at risk, would cause you to feel your very self was undermined? Any achievement, piece of your history, possession, relationship, physical or personality trait (positive or negative), body of expertise? Your manliness, your womanliness? Surely many things come to mind. A large, heavy basket full of things that define you. You carry this basket with you everywhere you go, every step up that sandy mountain. Your sense of self is a mighty burden, and the more you believe it's what you deeply are, the more susceptible you are to suffering.

Something in the mind of the invented self protests, *But how could it be otherwise? What would life mean if I weren't defined in some way?* The insistent objection speaks of the depth of identification, the near impossibility of imagining that there's something to you—something substantial and alive and juicy—that has *nothing* to do with all you identify with.

Here are some of the things that collected in my particular basket, whose ungainly weight I labored under for fifty years:

- The need to be right
- Intelligence
- Skill with language
- Being a Catholic, then a former Catholic
- Liberal political views
- Being attractive
- The loss of my father to an early death
- Wanting to be a good mother (but not always succeeding)
- Ideas about how the world should run
- Disappointment in love relationships
- The ability to befriend wild animals
- Musical aptitude
- The dread of not being thought well of
- The need to excel at all things undertaken
- Terror of death

I could go on. Do I need to? The wonder is that I didn't collapse under the weight of it. (Well, I did, when I had what used to be known as a nervous breakdown, unable to function for some months, when I was in my thirties.)

This is the nature of life. Carry, collapse, get up, trundle along, fall again. Until the final fall, from which there's no getting up.

What's in your basket?

What do you imagine other people say
when they describe you?

What have you accomplished
that you're really proud of?

What are you not so good at?

Learning About Your Familiar Self

What's illuminating, and liberating, is to gently but unflinch-ingly observe how you create yourself. The beliefs and values, the occupation or profession, the knowledge accumulated. The stories told (and retold) of what's happened in your life. How you suppose others see you. What you take pride in. All of it is carried along as you go from moment to moment. The cultiva-tion of a sense of self is an ongoing creation. The self, like life, is constantly in flux, even as it gives the impression of continuity, of solidity.

None of it is bad—or good. It's just the natural way a person goes about being a person. There's no need to try to stop it from happening. (You can't, anyhow.)

If you want to stop being at the mercy of life, the idea is to observe the functioning of the person-maintenance. Learn where you derive your sense of who you are. Watch yourself in a moment when you experience enhancement or threat to your identity. Listen to yourself tell a story about your history, or your present life, and see how real it all seems—to you and (as it appears) to your listener. How much it seems to matter, to be about what you fundamentally are. See too how frail it is, how very susceptible to undermining. See how much of what happens is taken personally, and therefore seriously. How anything that threatens your reputation, your well-being, your family, your possessions, your ideas is perceived as threatening to *you*.

Realize that this impression of self (however much pleasure and fulfillment it may bring) is an ultimately artificial thing, a mind-made construct that a huge amount of energy is devoted to upholding. Realize, too, that it's because of this real-seeming self that the liberated, radically *un*-identified presence within you is so seldom experienced. It's not only because of the extent of identification, but also because so much of it operates without your recognizing it for what it is. It's the *unrecognized* identification that most profoundly imprisons a person. Hence, the value of discovering it everywhere you can. What is *seen* has been stepped outside of.

If you were to awaken, all that you've believed yourself to be would fade from significance. The facts would still be there (the history, the roles, the personal traits), but you would cease to define yourself by them.

Suffering is able to happen because people identify not with radically allowing presence but with a self that's subject to threat. Change is constant. Some of what comes along is perceived as beneficial to that self, and some as compromising. The "self" that's without limiting identity doesn't experience the flow of life's ups and downs as either beneficial or detrimental. It's simply *life*.

When you're in the middle of something upsetting or gratifying, your perception probably isn't that *this is happening to my familiar self*. At such a moment, so absolute is the identification that you have no awareness of being anything *but* that person. The realization that there's more to you, that the egoic self exists in the mind, is something that might come later (if at all). But in the thick of a gripping moment of life experience, you've stepped into the body of that invented person and are moving within it, looking through its eyes, processing the present experience via all your accumulated understanding and propensities.

As a spiritual seeker, you may "know better" than to do this, aware that none of your narrow identity is "who you really are." But knowing better is of little use. In actual fact, as you experience day-to-day life, injury to any of your self-definition is felt as an injury to your very self. Anytime something brings satisfaction or draws praise to you and your good name, you feel as if it's *you* that's been enhanced.

The task, then, as you watch yourself live and experience, alternately beaming and wincing, is to discover what about yourself you deeply identify with. So that you can learn how the ongoing creation and care of your oh-so-real-seeming self takes place.

The more you see it functioning—*without attempting to change it*—the less ferociously it will hold you in its grip. When you begin to see how strongly you associate with your true nature what are ultimately mind-made things, the felt need to protect and maintain them will gradually, gently relax its terrible hold. Life will come to be not always about you, not always "good" or "bad," but instead just *life*.

Along the way, you'll be more able to sense the presence that underlies and surrounds the whole enthralling charade.

If these narrow definitions of self lead to so much suffering, why (you may wonder) does a person work so hard to keep that self going? Why identify with anything at all? It's because our early years, the world we're born into, and the self-reflective mind all collaborate to produce an ego. The ego needs a way to define itself, to help itself seem substantial and important. It becomes so large and dense a thing that it compels the belief in its reality, obscuring any possible view of that other thing we are—the longing for which fuels the spiritual life.

When you look in a full-length mirror,
how do you feel about what you see?

Is there anything about your physical
or mental condition that defines you,
or that gives you a way
to relate to others like you?

What roles do you play at home,
at work, in the community?

How important is your economic situation
in defining who you are?

Does your name have particular meaning to you?

Do you identify with your astrological sign?

How You Got to Be You

Your sense of who you are is significantly shaped by your conditioning. You experience life the way you do in large part because of the influence of previous experience. Conditioning is ongoing: it continues to shape who you are, and it will likely continue throughout the rest of your life.

When conditioning takes place, it means you're affected by having been subjected to something, whether that "condition" was a discrete experience or some kind of ongoing circumstance. You've taken on something of the condition itself; its effect has been incorporated into who you are.

When air is conditioned, it comes into the presence of a cooling-and-drying machine. The air has now taken on those traits. The machine conditioned the air, and now the air conditions the people, whose comfort is enhanced. When hair is conditioned, it's subjected to a substance that alters its texture and manageability. The hair is different from what it would have been without having come into contact with the goo in the bottle.

Life does the same thing to human beings. Unfolding developments change us, and from that point forward, we're different from what we were before. The conditioning may be seen as an improvement, or it may be seen as negative.

Most often, conditioning is not *seen* at all.

In Miami in the early 1960s, the neighborhoods were entirely segregated. The one my family lived in was all white people. One day some laborers came with bulldozers to work in the wooded lot beside our house. One of the men, seeing me in the yard, walked over and asked if he might have a drink of water. He was African-American—"colored," in those days. When I went inside to tell my mother, she rummaged around in the back of a cupboard and took out an empty peanut-butter jar and filled it with water. I was maybe ten, old enough to wonder at such things. (*We* never drank from jars.) My mother's response to the confused look on my face was to say, "I'm sorry, I can't help it."

As I matured, and the civil rights movement gathered momentum, putting me in school alongside kids from distant neighborhoods, I began to chafe against the racism I observed in many of my elders (and some of my peers), priding myself on my own relative open-mindedness.

Eventually, I would see that my mother, having grown up when and where she did, in fact could not (in some sense) "help it." No more than I could help being conditioned by the times I was born into, in which racism was brought into the light and examined. Since it probably wouldn't have occurred to my mother to examine the underlying beliefs that fueled her squeamishness, she literally couldn't help feeling that the laborer's mouth was unclean in a way our own mouths were not. Similarly, I couldn't help being more open-minded, growing up when I did, because of coming to know and care for kids who were dark-skinned—an experience, a *condition*, my mother had never been subjected to. The fact that I was being subjected to "good" conditioning, which let me see that people are people, didn't make me any less conditioned than my mother (however much credit I took for my greater tolerance). The conditioning of the times might have been fair-minded, but it was conditioning just the same. I could no more take credit for my tolerance than my mother could reasonably be held to account for her own deeply ingrained bias.

The very conditioning that was so favorably shaping my value system had its downside too: it made me squirm inside when, in later years, I felt racist assumptions stirring within myself. As vivid as the childhood memory of handing that man his jar of water, my eyes meeting his, are those later times of reckoning—terrible, guilty, secret. In the uneasy collision between ideals and the residue of racism, my liberal conditioning didn't help me during profoundly private moments of conflict. If anything, it made it more difficult to confront my lingering racism. The value system I wanted to believe was *me* was a place to take refuge—to hide from a deeply felt reaction that didn't line up with the humane ideals I espoused.

How would you describe your value system?

What position or opinion have you ardently upheld, or argued over?

What are your political views?

What are your spiritual or religious beliefs?

How Conditioning Works

The culture, family, and times you were born into have everything to do with the person you've turned out to be; had you
been born into different circumstances, you would be substan-
tially a different person. Every significant experience you've had
has probably altered you, subtly or noticeably. You come away
with a new belief (about how life works, about who you are),
or something you already understood has been reinforced, and
you're more sure than before that *this is how it goes*. Something
negative happens, and after that, you half expect it will happen
again. If you're assaulted in a city, afterward your feeling about
cities will likely be different from what it was before. If you have
a near-death experience, you may no longer fear death. If your
experience of people is that they're basically good, you're more
likely to trust people in general than if you've been hurt many
times. If you've had one painful relationship after another, you
may be reluctant to get involved again.

Some of what defines a person, unwittingly, are the awful
things done, the failings, the crimes of omission. The hurtful
thing you once said to your parent, and ever after, something in
you felt deeply cruel. The guilty knowing you feel more kin-
ship with one of your children than the other, and so you define
yourself as a bad parent.

Surely each of us has been shaped by our genetic inheritance. Some believe that their familiar selves are affected by prior
lives, or by the astrological circumstances surrounding the time
and place of their birth. It isn't important to assess the truth or
degree of these forces. Even if your conditioning is understood
to include the influence of heavenly bodies or karma, the essential self is independent of any of it. Moreover, that unconditioned
self doesn't experience reality in terms of beliefs (about the stars
or anything else). The significant thing is to see to what extent
you *identify* with anything you believe has shaped who you are.

Whatever influences there are, whatever circumstances you've been in, you take on understanding, values, inclinations, and needs as a result. Your accumulated experience becomes like a lens to look through. It informs choices that are made. Conditioning is a way the past gets carried forward into the present. It's how you continue developing into the person you are, day after day, year after year. You define yourself in the light of steadily accumulating learning from life as it's lived.

The sum of your conditioning enables you to know how to look at new experience, to apply to yourself what's happening, to protect yourself and all you value, to keep your bearings in a challenging situation. You revisit what you believe in, what you've learned.

Much of the conditioning that operates now was set in motion a long time ago, and has been with you for so long that it may escape your notice, even as you're working at becoming more self-aware. Although your processing of new experience inevitably is shaped by your conditioning, because of the long-standing and deeply entrenched nature of the forces that have formed your interpretive "lenses," your *awareness* of the ongoing process of interpretation will come and go. You aren't typically aware of conditioning *as conditioning,* either when it's initially set in motion or later, when its impact influences how you experience subsequent life. Of course, the more highly invested you are in retaining a defining feature of yourself— that is, the more strongly identified you are with your history and beliefs—the less likely you are to recognize it as conditioning. Chances are good that the stronger your reaction to an experience, the more powerful is the conditioning at play (and the stronger your resistance to acknowledging how it drives the reaction).

It's human nature to be shaped by experience. It's part of learning how to survive. The developing sense of self is also a way of saying what you are *not*—how you differ from others.

All of a person's history, viewed one way, is simply a series of events, things that have occurred. Plain facts. But we don't leave it at that. We let our life experience define us. We carry stories about it, telling them as many times as we can find someone to listen. The question is, *What would it be like to have had all your life experiences, to do all you do in the world, to be who you appear to be, and yet not let it all define you?*

My father died when I was eighteen. For years, I thought of myself as someone who became fatherless barely out of childhood. I defined myself by that loss. As the years went on, I tended to automatically contrast my experience with that of my friends who still had their fathers. When I got married and there was no father to walk me up the aisle, I felt sorry for myself. Of course it would be natural to wish my father were there. But that's different from carrying a story (all the way up the aisle) about *being* a fatherless bride.

It can look as though significant experience clings to *us*. That there's no choice in the matter of whether to carry it ahead into subsequent life. Yet we hold tightly to our defining experiences, not because we couldn't put them down, but because we don't *want* to: they seem to be who we are. Little do we suspect they don't hold on to us, but instead we hold them tight in our fists.

The tendency to define self in terms of experience is most potent when it's something that's caused a deep wounding, or that's left a reservoir of outrage or self-loathing. Yet all the while, what happened did not happen to the true self. Something was not wounded. Something emerged from even the most devastating experience untouched, unaffected.

How do you imagine your childhood friends and
teachers remember you?

What is your cultural or ethnic heritage?

What have you not gotten over?

What stories about yourself
do you tell again and again?

The Value of Seeing Your Identity in Action

The reason to notice your conditioned responses, to see your
identity in action, is so you can learn how the ego keeps itself
going. It's so you can become more attuned to that presence
within that isn't affected by what happens. To observe identification in action asks for an undefended willingness to really
look at yourself, from a bit of a distance.

Who are you without your conditioning? What's left, if you
take away all of that? What in you hasn't been conditioned, is
not subject to circumstance and experience?

You don't need to get rid of all you identify with in order
not to suffer. You need only to notice it functioning. Everything you think of as *you*—every scrap of it—is overlaid on the
emptiness that's your essential nature. The conditioned self is an
idea-of-yourself. It's ultimately artificial, existing (only) in your
mind, however objectively real it may feel to you (or appear to
others) in any given moment. It moves through life feeling like
the center of its private universe, looking at whatever happens
to see if or how it's relevant to the self that has desires and fears,
that hopes things turn out a certain way, that takes pride in what
it does, that has a sense of who it is, a sense of what it needs to
keep itself in good shape.

The more you see this, in life as it's actually lived, the lighter a load you will carry.

In honest inquiry, you're likely to become increasingly aware of how you've been shaped by experience. Things you've taken for granted as being simply "who you are" are brought into the light. You'll become more alert to the things that push your buttons, that you heavily identify with, that "cause" you in some way to resort to an unconscious response. You may become less automatically subject to the force of those influences. Even as you feel the pull toward unconsciousness, you may be able to watch the process unfolding, perhaps not "going there" as wholeheartedly as in the past.

The value of discovering your identity attachments isn't so much to be able to tease apart all the nuances. It's simply to see that the mental/emotional arena is, by its nature, a conditioned place.

**What turning points in your life
have been significant?**

**What about your history made you
into the person you are?**

What was your family of origin like?

Identification That's Tricky to Recognize

It seems natural, expected—maybe even admirable—to have beliefs and values about important issues. Most any thoughtful person holds particular views about politics, the environment, social trends, the arts, business, religion, and world events. Many seekers hold deeply considered spiritual beliefs.

The more widely approved, eccentric, or lofty a belief, the more tempting it may be to derive a sense of self from it—and the harder it is to recognize identification at play. Justice, compassion, and a sense of responsibility are universally regarded as virtues. The more generally acknowledged as *good* a given stance or behavior, the more challenging it can be to see that you derive a sense of self from it. It isn't about whether a point of view is "right" or valid, whether the work you do and the ideals you stand for are worthy. It's that you can take worthwhile action and live in accord with your values *without defining yourself by them*.

If you're willing to be truthful with yourself, you may see that your embracing of beliefs is done at least in part *because* that association creates a sense of identity. When you espouse ideas seen as admirable or virtuous, you may thereby feel ennobled. Believing in something, especially when it's outwardly expressed, is a way of saying *this is who I am; I'm someone who believes thus-and-so*. It can provide a way of being in the world, of relating to others. The more noble or beneficial a role you assume in your work, family, or community, the trickier it can be to tease apart the *action itself* from the sense of self it helps define.

It takes rigorous spiritual integrity to recognize the temptation to draw a sense of self from what you do, what you believe in, what you're good at. The willingness to acknowledge identification will open a door to freedom and ease that greatly exceeds whatever you might have felt was gained from taking on positive roles and beliefs.

Even when it's in the realm of something "spiritual," or something worthy of emulation, identification is a way of supporting the egoic self. Identifying with a loving stance can be every bit as imprisoning as embodying mean-spirited, small-minded bigotry. A person can be just as attached to an open-hearted viewpoint as to a nasty one. Any cultivated identity keeps freedom at a distance.

You may have a particular spiritual practice or orientation, and it may be a great support in your deepening awareness. But it isn't necessary (or helpful) to *define* yourself as a practitioner. Self-definition draws you further from your higher self, not closer to it.

Sometimes a painful piece of a person's history, or an ongoing challenge in present-day life, will give rise to an identification that's profound. A consuming condition (such as an addiction, or a chronic or terminal illness) or a devastating prior experience (abandonment, victimization) may result in rigid self-definition. There may be a deeply ingrained reluctance to acknowledge the identification—*because to release it would be to experience a diminishing of self.*

The fact of what happened, or of what you're presently facing, is one thing—perhaps challenging, absorbing, life-altering. *Defining* yourself by it is another. You cannot undo reality. But it *is* possible to recognize that you're deriving your sense of who you are from this thing that happened, or that's happening now. The challenge is to explore how to be with the painful reality while not identifying it as your very self. The pain of the real situation is already considerable; it's only exacerbated by drawing a sense of self from it, because a painful identity makes it difficult to be okay *anyhow.*

The challenge—one that asks enormous courage—is to see that you *are* identifying with the difficult truth. You may think, *This thing is so severe, so damaging, that it's truly what I* am. A deeply buried thought underlies the identification: *To not identify is to say the thing doesn't matter.* As if to allow the identification to soften would amount to minimizing the facts or the pain they've caused. Yet allowing the identification to ease up would ease the suffering, enabling you to see the distinction between what happened and what you *are.*

It's one thing to have suffered abuse as a child. It's another to define yourself, the rest of your life, as an abuse survivor.

Another buried idea might be this one: *At least, if I have suffered so terribly, I can derive a sense of self from it.* If this thought is there, it's likely not operating at the conscious level. The need for a self runs so deep that the ego willingly takes it wherever it may be found, even in what is excruciating.

If you want to be free of what has defined you, if you want to stop suffering, the first step is to see how you cling to it as being who you are. Once you feel how hard you hold on to it, there's some hope of letting it go.

When you cease identifying with your condition, or your history, you may find you're less fixated on setting things right, recovering, solving problems. No longer is so much riding on a resolution, because you no longer believe that to fix things would be to fix *you*. Once you no longer identify with your issues (even if they are ongoing, perhaps severe), they will cease to imprison you.

If you can live without constant reference to your past, your present condition, your ideas and values, you'll be freer to experience reality freshly—to sense your higher (unconditioned) self in the presence of it. To really be present. And the less you'll experience what happens as being about you—even when something you've identified with takes a hit. You'll suffer less.

Do you derive a sense of identity
from your spiritual practice?

Do you notice yourself acting
"spiritual" in certain settings?

Do you define yourself as a survivor,
an addict, a victim?

Seeing Identity in Motion

Learning about your identity can occur anytime you notice yourself strongly affected by what's happening, when you're roused to some kind of energetic response. The moment seems to reinforce or challenge something about yourself.

Be alert to patterned responses, familiar ways of believing or judging, that seem to start up on their own. The lens each person looks through is uniquely personalized, and at first seems to be the only way to see, to experience. Until, that is, you step outside of it and watch yourself in the scene. In momentary observation, it becomes possible to see your identity as the "pre-fabricated" thing it is.

Thinking you know about people and phenomena is one of the ways the sense of self is maintained. When your understanding of something familiar is compromised, you may feel subtly threatened, reluctant to relax or adapt the accustomed idea. If, for instance, your sister (whom you haven't seen for a while) speaks or behaves in a way that deviates from your long-held view of her, your ability to really see who she is now may be hampered by those predetermined expectations, based on your long experience with her.

As you watch your identity express itself, you've stepped to the side; you're looking *at* it rather than through its eyes. You can see conditioning at play—if you can manage to let down your inner guard. There's no need to psychoanalyze yourself, to attempt to trace the source of the "self" being stirred to life (an exhausting exercise, and not of much use). All that's needed is to see your sense of self in motion.

In this observation, you may experience a subtle spaciousness around the moment, a sense of freedom that wouldn't have been there, had you allowed the familiar to assert itself unobserved. You're getting a taste of what it is to not allow narrow definitions to determine your experience of the now, but rather to occupy the moment freshly and fully—to experience yourself as *part of* what-is, rather than at a discerning distance from it, as if you were somehow apart from life itself. Backing away from the moment and seeing yourself in it increases the likelihood of experiencing the presence of your deeper self. Because the one doing the seeing is beyond the conditioning. It encounters reality directly, without any tendency to interpret, resist, cling. When you aren't attached to ideas of who you are (or at least can see you *are* attached), you realize there's more to you.

Sometimes the observation may happen only afterward. On reflection, you may realize that a potent reaction (anger, jumping to conclusions, stereotyping) seems to have been stirred by a piece of your history, or something that matters to you now.

It's sometimes said that when an addict is under the influence, it's the substance that's talking or behaving, not the authentic person underneath. So it is with the familiar self. When you allow belief and identity attachment to run you, you are essentially "under the influence." It's the mind-made persona—not the real you—that's reacting. Once you see that, it begins to be possible to be free of it.

After a time, you may wonder what would remain if your defined self were magically to dissolve. You may see how much of what you think of as *you* is ultimately insubstantial. Your sense of self may become a softer, lighter thing, not in such constant need of vigilance and upkeep.

You can't go back in time and undo all that's made you into who you are. But you *can* see it for what it is. When you see the familiar self for what it is, you no longer have to be at the mercy of it.

If my mother could have seen that she was the product of the times she grew up in, maybe she could have seen past that man's blackness to simply imagine his dry mouth, his thirst not unlike her own. Maybe she could have gotten him a *glass* of water. And if I could have understood that my more open-minded orientation was something granted by my own times and circumstances, then later, in those deeply private moments when I felt the presence of racism, I might have been able to really see that (and to see that it, too, had its roots in conditioning). I might have been more understanding, more forgiving, of the racism I observed in my mother and others.

When you see how thoroughly you've been shaped by your life experience, it's inevitable you'll come to see others in the same light of understanding. None of us can "help" it. In this recognition, compassion flowers naturally. We're all at the mercy of what life has been like. Seeing conditioning at play, in self and in others, doesn't constitute an excuse for bad behavior (nothing relieves anyone of responsibility). It does yield a truer understanding than the one that supposes our differences are innate, or something to be proud or ashamed of, rather than simply an outcome.

What values did you learn in your youth?

How are you different from what you used to be?

New Conditioning

Much of experience amounts to simple reinforcement of already-established conditioned views. But new conditioning is set in motion all the time, particularly in connection with a significant life event—something that hits hard, that represents a turning point, such as a major disappointment or success, a dramatic change in circumstances. Being conscious during life-changing experience may prevent new conditioning from taking hold, and it also enables a vivid real-time view of how the ego is molded.

After all, much of your present identity originated in *some* present-tense moment. Some formative experience affected you in such a way that you took away a lasting impression. If you'd been thinking to notice at the time—to recognize what was happening as conditioning-in-progress—the shaping influence of the experience on your subsequent life and identity may not have been as pronounced.

In a time of significant change, perhaps with something unnerving in the picture (a serious accident, being served divorce papers), you may observe yourself thinking, *Now that this has happened, from now on I will . . .* or *This means I am no longer . . .* or *I guess I was wrong to think I would always. . . .* You may notice a wish to predict or influence the course of subsequent developments. There's a potent discomfort with anything unpredictable or uncontrollable, a feeling of urgency to come to a conclusion about how life has changed, to reinterpret the past in the light of the new developments. You want to revise your understanding of how the world operates. Previously held beliefs feel threatened or no longer applicable, so you cast about to discover sources of security, the old ones no longer reliable. These various forms of scrambling to get your bearings are indications that the machinery of conditioning is in high gear. Your egoic self is anxious to know what it all means for you.

As you watch yourself search for solid ground to stand on, you'll get to observe a process that's gone largely unobserved your entire life, something that until now you've experienced only the outcome of, long after the fact: the ingraining of conditioning.

If you can experience something big without having your sense-of-self redefined, you're letting the past be the past. You're able to move forward unburdened by what's happened. Note that burden hasn't only to do with the residue of *negative* experience; it applies just as well to something favorable. *Wow, I'm the CEO of my company now!* Or, having been declared cured, *I'm no longer a person with cancer. I'm a survivor.* The altered identity carried forward from a significant moment has just as much "weight" with a positive experience as with a difficult one. It becomes something (yet another something) to carry into your subsequent experience, a piece of identity to define yourself by, to maintain, a thing in the light of which new developments will be interpreted. All of it keeps the ego going.

When you're at one of these crossroads, ask yourself what it would feel like to move forward without carrying any residue from what's happened. What is it to experience something big without letting it significantly color your sense of who you are?

It isn't as though you can't learn from experience. New insights can come that may inform future choices. But learning can happen without entrenchment in a new belief system or identity.

Since coming to know what you essentially are asks for a readiness to let go of the conditioned self, certainly you'd do well not to take on any new definitions. What's called for is a gentle, steady *undoing*. Becoming more awake to what you really are isn't a matter of replacing old constructs with new ones. It's about letting go the need to have any at all.

You don't have to keep the pattern going. There's nothing that says you must be changed by even significant experience. If you can simply move forward, free of burden, you'll be able to engage what's next in a way that's free of resistance, fear, and limiting ideas. You'll be better able to be present, to discover the you that's not bound to suffer.

Crisis as an Opening

A challenging event that undermines your sense of security can bring about a spiritual opening, because it threatens or destroys something about yourself or your life that you've counted on as solid and reliable. A crisis exposes the egoic self as the flimsy thing it always was. So while you're swirling in feelings of loss and instability, be alert to the possibility of real inner change, to the relaxing of lifelong patterns. Just at the moment when you might be tempted to cast about for new ideas of who-you-are, for some kind of guidance system for moving forward, instead, allow yourself to dwell in the sensation of being unmoored.

Rather than being drawn into new conditioning, feel what it is to simply be in the presence of changing circumstances.

Stay with the opportunity brought about by the difficult situation. Your ego has taken a hit. The pain is a sign that your familiar self is no longer functioning the same. From the point of view of awakening to your true nature, this can only be seen as a blessing.

The familiar self is so substantial that it may yield only to a severe blow. Sometimes it takes extremity to cause a person to ask, *Who am I without all this?*

What things about yourself generate a sense of security and well-being?

What's the most recent life experience that significantly altered your perspective?

Ongoing Creation, Ongoing Opportunity

Just as your ego ceaselessly creates itself, you constantly have the option to do things differently from how you've done them before. The potential for freedom is newly alive again and again. Whatever the burden of the past, however deeply entrenched the patterns of identification, each moment it becomes possible to look afresh—at yourself, at your orientation to your history and beliefs, at the presence of what-is. Each moment holds the shimmering possibility to experience yourself as *awareness*, as part of the immediacy of life itself, rather than as a solidly defined somebody bound to take on residue from what happens.

What if you had no name for the sort of person you are? No category for yourself, no defining feature that distinguished you from others?

But people *like* to call themselves things. *Mystic, survivor, Scorpio, grandmother, dreamer.* Always the clawing desperation to be a something. *Artist, intellectual, family man.* Even if it's painful, or negative. *Ex-con, addict, abuser, loser.*

The piling on of identities, personae. A way of being somebody, of naming that for others so they know who you are. A way to be sure you exist.

What is it to wake up? One thing it means is to let all of your "somebody-ness" drop away. None of it means anything anymore. Waking up is the great *un*-defining, the negating of selfhood. Which is one of the reasons it doesn't happen every day—why it would be easy to live an entire life and never encounter a single person who was undefined.

People enjoy their identities.

When you awaken, you realize you are everything that is. And nothing at all. You are flexible, porous, welcoming, yielding. Nothing is any longer riding on something. You're stuck to nothing that ever happens. Rigidity has run in a trickle down the drain. You can stand softly for anything. Lightened, you can move with ease, be anywhere, look from any perspective. It's as if you could fly.

Who are you? If you're lucky, it becomes a question to make you laugh. Absurd, silly, the idea of being-a-something, a certain somebody. Why, if you have ceased being afraid, ceased clinging, ceased seeking meaning—why, please, would you wish to take on limiting definition?

It's all about taking off the costumes, one after the other. However pretty and reassuring and dignifying they've been.

In this life you are given, you can go one direction or the other: ever more costumes, ever more ornately and heavily decorated, or the open sky. It's up to you.

But here's a clue: you don't get to play dress-up when it's time to die.

The time to die is now. While you've still got time to live.

Part Three

The Solitary Traveler, with No Place to Go

If there were a spiritual journey,
it would be only a quarter inch long.

—JOHN O'DONOHUE

14

What Do You Want?

You've been living your life. Life has been living you, and as it's all been happening, you've been more and less resisting, more and less fearful, attached, aware. Increasingly, you're able to observe yourself neutrally. You notice conditioning asserting itself. Sometimes it's able to unwind, or at least to be steadily observed. Sometimes not (which may be observed, or not, in retrospect). The things you identify with have come more to be seen for what they are—except when they insist they really *are* what you are, and on those occasions you may have noticed pain (subtle or maybe not).

You see more clearly than before the things you do to keep your familiar self going. By now, it's somewhat less dense and substantial-seeming, with less energy devoted to narrowly defined efforts at self-preservation. Perhaps you're not as attached to your beliefs as before. You're more attuned to the mind's power to create an impression of reality, and less prone to buy into it. Maybe you're less defensive, because your sense of what you are (what would require defending) has lightened up a bit.

Surely your awareness is with the present more consistently than before. You see choice operating where previously you felt at the mercy of one thing and another. Not to say you always let choice flower. But maybe you at least see it (if through lids squeezed nearly shut).

More remains to be seen. If, that is, you keep the doors and windows open. If, that is, you remain willing to see. To let go. To be undone, unnerved. If you welcome the prospect of being relieved of burden. Of being tilted toward freedom.

All of this that you open yourself to—this willingness to see yourself, to yield to what-is, even to the uncomfortable—has delivered you into an existence where suffering doesn't have you by the nape of the neck. Where you sense more and more the presence of your essential being. Less focused on maintaining a solid self, you're softer in the presence of reality, feeling your "self" as simply a part of all that is.

It's a fine place to be—finer by far than the old place, wherein you bought into the idea that if you could just achieve the right circumstances and personal traits, you might be happy and secure. Note that the reduction in suffering has not come about, necessarily, by any improvement in your situation. As ordinary life continues to feel more comfortable, see that the outer condition may continue unchanged.

This inner condition of greater ease lends itself to the ever-deepening consideration of what life's about, anyway—the question of what is the nature of a human being. What's possible, ultimately, for you, in your very life.

It may be time to revisit the question of what you most deeply want: to feel better (on the level of the familiar self), or to know the ultimate truth? What do you ask of life—of your beloved self—in this time that you have, however long that may be?

What if today were it? Really? (One fine day it will be, you know.) What would you ask of existence? How would you spend the precious drop of life you're given?

What if—within this life—there were no end, no limit to how far you could go? Into what? Into freedom, emptiness, joy. Life delighting in its own presence, in your very body. No space for problems. Nothing tight, nothing lonely or bewildered.

What if it could be? Doesn't matter what's happened so far, or what hasn't. Doesn't matter what your condition is. How old, how unseasoned, how caught up you may be.

It's as close as the next beat of your heart.

It's right here.

●

I'm speaking to you now as though you want to be done with illusion.

Do you want freedom enough to stick with it? Do you want it instead of all other things? (You may have to ask yourself this question more than once.)

This is where you walk to the edge of the cliff that has been your life. This is where you get comfortable with being uncomfortable. Where you stop expecting to know the way, or even wishing to.

The willingness to discover your own complicity in your suffering has made life more of an adventure than a trial. Maybe it's made your "self" more the object of bemusement than angst. (One could only hope so.)

Maybe it's made the prospect of self-obliteration less like a nightmare and more like a curiosity.

The choice you face is to live as your mind-made egoic self or to live as presence. It's the difference between *self-having-experience* and *life-experiencing-itself*. Occupy the present moment as living awareness, or confront it as a bundle of thoughts. This choice plays itself out every moment you live.

No one can tell you how to get there. If it matters enough to you, you'll do what it takes.

But somebody who is there *can* make suggestions about where to look, and where not to look, and where to look from.

If you're ready to go on, then go. Like a maniac.

What is it to be ready to go for broke? It's to be that drowning person desperate for one gulp of air.

If you're not ready, it's okay. (Doesn't mean you won't ever be.)

What you need to get is that the gate of your prison cell is not locked. It doesn't need to be: your fingers are curled around a bar, gripping, pulling hard with all your weight. No wonder you can't get out. (Think of it: desperate for freedom, and all this devotion to holding the gate closed.)

A person does not want to know this: that she is keeping herself at a distance from liberation. That the prisoner and the jailer are the same is a most unwelcome truth. But it must be turned toward, if you want it to be otherwise. You must find out what you do, moment to moment, to keep yourself believing you are that mind-made person. Or else just get comfortable where you are, rearranging the furniture in the cell.

Maybe you haven't even realized how you've been holding on to that bar. Are you tired? Maybe that's where to start. Feel how exhausted you are from working to keep yourself enclosed in that tiny cage full of ideas of who you are. When the gate would swing liquidly on its hinges, if you'd just let go.

Only, there'd be nobody there to walk out. When you let go, you cease to be.

What if you were a thought in your own head?

It's all got to do with where you're looking from. That's the whole thing. Wherever you're used to looking from, bring yourself to look from a slightly different angle, so the light shines differently on the thing you're looking at. So the shadows fall an unfamiliar way.

Don't be in a rush to hurry back to the place you're accustomed to looking from.

There's another way to think of this. It's got to do with which one of "you" is doing the looking. Are you looking with the eyes of the egoic self, or with the eyes of presence? Both are available to you. You can tell the difference. One of them has an agenda, and discomfort. The other is entirely at rest.

When you don't get something, it just means you're not ready to get it. You're not (yet) looking from the perspective where it's possible to clearly see. You may be looking with the wrong eyes. It doesn't mean you'll never get it. When you're ready to, you will. (You know how this goes. It's already happened probably: something you read or heard many times and never got for the longest time . . . until you finally did. Or something you *thought* you understood, but later—having *really* gotten it—realized you'd only "known" it in your head. That will keep happening, if you're lucky.)

Meanwhile, don't imagine you can get it by *thinking* a little harder. You have to be standing in a place you're not yet standing to be able to see it. Seeing and thinking are not the same thing. Once you're there, you can't fail to see what's always been in plain sight.

Whenever thinking isn't called for, decline to think. Instead, attend. Stay conscious. Not in the world of thought, but tuned into what's real here now. Neglect everything else, but not this. Be constantly aware of what awareness is doing.

Keep attention on the looker, not on the looked-at.

Note the tendency to believe a thought. Any thought at all. To think thinking can lead someplace real.

Resist nothing, either inside or out. Turn toward, never away from. If you are conscious of being in resistance, realize there's something you want more than to wake up.

When you notice yourself caught in thought or emotion, do nothing with it. Just step outside and look at its happening. Do not indulge. Just walk beyond it, turn around, and look back. (There *is* a place beyond it. It's that perspective thing.)

There's no end of new places to stand, to look from.

If an emotion overtakes you and you can't step outside it, surrender to it for a bit (completely). Then try again.

Avert your eyes from nothing on your interior. Do not hide from yourself. See and feel what's there. Don't be afraid of yourself. Note any impulse to protect yourself from self-knowledge. If there's a part of your mind-made self that you secretly know you're keeping going (by avoiding looking), either take a deep breath and look directly at it or be truthful with yourself that waking up is not for you. Don't tell yourself there's some other option.

Decline to judge self. If you cannot observe yourself without judging, go back to square one. Learn how to do that, then come back here. (*Here* will wait for you.)

●

Be attuned to even the most subtle degree of suffering. Ask, *Who is it that's suffering?* Never tire of asking this. Either you can simply suffer, or you can ask who's doing it. The first choice will keep the suffering going forever. The second one gets you looking from another angle. (Note if you feel your grip on the prison gate relaxing when you look from someplace else than the usual.)

Do nothing whatsoever to keep time alive. Tune into moments when you do so: hope, regret, rehash, intend, expect. Ask, *Who is doing this?* and *What does it get me when I do it?* Note any tendency of the mind to believe that the past matters, or that the future is real. (Of course, you will still do things like schedule appointments. Don't get too literal here. We're looking at how the self keeps itself alive, at how the present is avoided.)

Give up the idea of being on a journey. *This is it.* This *now* is it. Note the tendency to hold on to any moment before this one. Stop. Drop it: now is here.

●

When you feel something mattering, ask, *Who does this matter to?* Step outside the thing (the mattering) and look at it. Just look. (Remember to wonder, *Who is looking?* None of it matters to the one who is looking.)

●

Don't get stuck in anything. Spiritual practice, perspective, ideas (including ideas about self, about awakening), plans, longing, fear, identity. Cease to believe in anything. Note the desire to want to be able to count on something. (Anything.) None of it is real anyplace besides your head.

Do not be spiritual. It doesn't work that way. (It's a good way to put your fingers in a perpetual cramp.)

Change doesn't happen by approximation, by cultivating qualities of what might look like the desired condition. Change doesn't come by trying to change yourself. It comes when you're willing to see where you actually are, however unspiritual that may be.

If you must be spiritual, do it until you see it isn't getting you anywhere. Then come back here. Or if you like it there, admit it's where you want to be and give this up.

Does regular life feel like a problem to you? Like it's in conflict with the spiritual life? Exactly where do you think the present moment is to be found?

Do you think of your spiritual life as being off to the side? An occasional focus of attention? Is your regular life a thing that gets in the way of your spiritual life?

Picture your regular life. Now picture your spiritual life. Do you see two different pictures? If each is painted on a piece of glass and you put one on top of the other, do they line up exactly?

Do you think if you wake up, you'll have spiritual times and regular times? If you can see the absurdity here, let this be a clue to you, where you are now, in your orientation to "regular" life.

The means and the end are not different. The way to wake up is to be awake. If you separate the spiritual from ordinary life, extracting things to do with conscious presence and dropping them into their own little beautiful category, you're forcing an artificial distinction where there isn't one. The distinction exists in your mind. It doesn't exist in the real world.

The love of spirituality brings about an inebriation guaranteed to keep you drowsy. Awakeness is sober. It moves *toward* life, not away from it. It isn't looking for escapes. It doesn't slip into heightened states to get away from difficulty. So you shouldn't either, while you're trying to be more awake than asleep. If you see the life of the spirit and the life of the good old earth as being anything but two different ways of saying the same thing, think again. That's a big part of your problem, if you wonder why you aren't awake.

Begin with this, and end with this: the present moment is it. It's all there is. It will never be otherwise. When you give yourself to the present moment, you sense the eternal that is your deep interior. Here, there is the felt oneness of the spiritual and whatever might have looked like the antithesis of the spiritual. In a living moment, separation is nonsensical.

Awareness in the act of feeling its aliveness, its beingness: that is the moment. That's life. That's *you*. That's the whole thing. It's the sensation of being awake. There's not a perceiver and a perceived. There's not a someone experiencing a something. It's the stroke of a paintbrush, all a single gesture: perceiver and perceived; doer and done; the thing happening and the setting in which it happens. It's all one thing: a happening. Life is never bigger than what constitutes a single moment.

When you run, there's no runner apart from the running. When you love, there's no lover apart from the love. When you take in a breath, the motion of the lungs can mean nothing apart from the moving air. The song doesn't exist until someone sings it. Song, singing, singer are all happening, and if you remove one, the whole thing ceases to be.

It's only in the mind that the whole can be teased apart into components, or that moments can be strung together into an image of "life."

Perceive your "self" this way. That supposedly substantial entity, with its objective-seeming reality. See that you *do not exist* apart from your aliveness this moment. Everything else you might think you are is a bundle of recollected thoughts.

What if the mind lost its capacity to remember? All you would ever know of yourself is the only thing there ever actually is: this, you, here, now. Again: this, you, here, now.

Can't you see?

How can you dream up the idea of a journey? Having a destination? Yet it drives a person mad to think, *What if it were true, that this moment is all there is?*

What if it were true?

The past and the future are thoughts in the mind. Where is life? When does *life* happen? When you take away the past and the future, what is left? What are you left with? Where are *you*?

Does having the past and the future taken away from you feel like getting backed into a tiny little cramped corner? *But they never were really real anyway.* A memory is not the same order of reality as a moment of life. How did the memories come about? Each one started as a moment of life. No memory could have started itself without an actual lived moment taking place.

A single drop of rainwater falling from a leaf into a pond. How many times does it touch? A thousand times it may be recollected, but only once did it release the leaf, drop, and touch.

That is it. There, right there. Can you see? That is where your life is lived.

The moment ripens and dissolves. You ripen and dissolve. What's happening ripens and dissolves. It's all one thing, life living itself. *Now:* the stroke of a luscious, moist paintbrush. That's the whole thing.

You can't have it over again. (The paint dries quickly.) But here: wait. You've got another! Life is a Pez dispenser. The moments just keep offering themselves to you.

Stop feeling sorry for yourself. You don't exist, except for right now. If you had no memories of previous moments, you could not feel sorry for yourself.

15

Spiritual Practice
as Distraction

You might, for a time, have a spiritual practice, if that's how you're naturally inclined. But don't curl up in it. Do you have the idea that if you become "spiritual" enough, you'll wake up? Maybe you do your spiritual practices (meditate, chant, attend retreats, do mindfulness practice, repeat mantras) as a way to escape painful things—like the inside of your head. Like difficult feelings, some piece of painful history, or challenging present-life circumstances (money worries, relationship problems, health issues). If you are in any way using your spiritual life to avoid real life, to protect you from feelings—from what you actually, deeply are (with all your unspiritual tendencies, if you're truthful with yourself)—take a hard look at what you're doing. Your spiritual practice should draw you *into* present-moment reality, not help you retreat from it.

Maybe being faithful with your practices gives you a way to feel good about yourself. Your already-awake self doesn't need anything to help it feel good about itself. Which means it's the ego-self that derives that particular satisfaction. If you want your ego to lose interest in itself, you must question these invitations into deepening illusion.

Supposing that awakeness is on a plane apart from ordinary existence, some seekers try to cultivate "spiritual" qualities and experiences as a way to sidestep life when it gets challenging. Achieving mystical experiences or psychic states may mean they're "getting close." Fueling devotion to a certain path or practice, these erroneous ideas detract attention from where it ought to be: on where you are, right now, in your real-life experience.

If you want to wake up, focus *not* on cultivating the characteristics you associate with awakeness, and *not* on attaining blissful states, and *not* on trying to be better than you are. Instead, let your attention be steadily on where you *are*. On reality.

If you wonder whether your spiritual practice is serving you, look to see if it keeps cracking you open, causing you to become less certain of who you are and what you know. Does your spiritual life feel more like a field of landmines or a feather bed?

The presence of your teacher may be like a balm, but is it ever undermining? This isn't an argument for seeking out an abusive or unkind teacher, or a tradition endorsing strenuous austerities. It's to say that if the teacher or practice is doing any good, you'll not only sense the truth there; you'll also be brought to confront yourself, unimpeded by belief, hope, or illusion.

Perhaps you notice how much better you're doing than before; you're more compassionate, less reactive. These are doubtless welcome developments, but if your attention is primarily on the impression of progress, you're living in the past, comparing who you used to be with who you are now.

There can be a great temptation to use spiritual understanding to avoid looking at your attachment to egoic identity, or to justify "letting it be," even as you acknowledge its presence. You may say, *It's okay that this happens, so long as I'm witnessing it,* or *It does no harm, since I know it isn't who I really am.* This kind of argument, which is based on understanding that's mental only, will do nothing to liberate you. It will keep you at a distance from reality. Sound asleep.

Do you derive an identity from your spiritual practice? Do you identify with your tradition, your sangha, spiritual routines, teacher? Do you have a spiritual name that seems to define you? You may have a social life or some other significant context with others doing the same practice. Perhaps your sense of self is shaped by the association with others following the same teacher, having a spiritual frame of reference in common with you. Maybe you want so much to be like those you admire that you actually pretend to be something you're not (like patient, when you're secretly irritated and judgmental).

It will all take you only so far. It may even help you stay stuck. (An identity that's "spiritual" is still an identity. Awakened presence identifies with *nothing*.) At some point, if you mean to be emptied out and delivered into the truth of what you essentially are, you'll very likely cease to depend on a spiritual practice.

Having a path can make sense for a time—until it no longer does.

It's not that spiritual practices and beliefs don't sometimes support eventual awakening. It's that people tend to get stuck there. They make little circles within their idea of themselves as being practitioners of a certain tradition. Any truly worthwhile practice or teacher will eventually render itself useless. The purpose of these spiritual supports is not to engender dependence, and certainly not to provide comfort. Any legitimate teacher will tell you that right upfront. A spiritual practice is not meant to define a way of life for you. (Or if it is that, you'd do well to realize it, and maybe let go of the idea that what you want is liberation.)

The questions about truth, finally, must be posed by you, to yourself. A spiritual practice can point the way; it can teach you ways to increase self-awareness. But it cannot go with you into your interior as you live, into the moment-to-moment of your existence, the fabulously complex structure you've erected and maintained over decades to keep you believing you're the person you seem to be. A person with problems, with a history, with frustrated desires. A person who wants freedom from suffering, but cannot see how the constant derailing of fulfillment is an inside job.

16

A Jewel in Your Pocket

The one that wants so much to know, that thinks it understands something, is the one that ceases to believe in itself upon awakening.

If you want a sign (unmistakable as neon) that you're operating within the egoic self, anytime you think you know something, or wish you did, you can be certain it's the ego that's thinking this. This is the very self that won't feel real anymore after you wake up. So don't indulge it. If you get caught up in thinking you've mastered something, or in wishing you could, recognize that it's the ego-mind having that thought. Just say, *There it is again.*

The experience of being on a spiritual journey sometimes includes a moment of knowing, clear seeing into the truth of something. Such a moment can give rise to a wanting to hold on to what's been seen, to carry it like a jewel in your pocket. So it can be fingered later for reassurance, in a time of bewilderment.

But no. Collect no jewels in your pocket.

The one that would load up the pocket with jewels is the one that ceases to believe in itself upon awakening.

The tree does not wish to understand or to know.

See what the mind does with that. *But a human being is not a plant,* it protests. *A tree doesn't have the capacity for intelligence.*

This is not an argument for going stupid, or for pretending people are just like trees.

When your pockets are heavy, and your fingers are busy revisiting the accumulated things, you've put yourself at a distance from the living thing *this moment* is. You just can't be making reference to a prefabricated interpretive idea and at the same time being with what-is. You're either in your head or you are being.

A moment you're awake to is just itself. It's not you *in some orientation to it.* As soon as the moment begins to *mean* something, you're gone from it.

So, the tree.

The difference between a tree and a person is that the person is able to watch itself be. This isn't just thinking-about. Thinking-about is at a remove. This is about being, and knowing that you be, simultaneously. The mind, then, is quiet.

Some adults recall the youthful moment of original self-awareness. *I exist, and I see myself knowing this.* The primal existential recognition.

Awakeness is about that. Something in us never forgets what that felt like, what that *feels* like, to experience the utterly thrilling sensation of being. Pure being—absent any meaning—simply feeling itself be.

Like a tree exists. That kind of pure being. Only the tree, so far as we can tell, cannot self-reflect. It cannot know that it *is.*

We can. You can.

But it's not thinking that brings this to awareness. Observe how it feels to *think-about-something.* To finger the bead in the pocket, for instance. To trot out a previously understood thing and apply it *here.* Or to try to go back *there,* to the moment that thing first got understood. There's process there; there's movement. There's something invested in knowing, interpreting, synthesizing. Progressing.

It's quite another thing to *feel-yourself-be*.

A teacher worth his salt will not load you up with jewels but instead will secretly take a seam ripper to one corner of your pocket, so that every time you're tempted to take something he says and drop it into your pocket, when your fingers go looking later, they'll find an empty pocket, and be thrown back into the present.

The finger may discover the hole, worrying it the way a tongue does a missing tooth. It may try to plug it, as if the pocket were a leaky dike. But then the hand must be devoted to the pocket, and is not available for clapping or for playing baseball.

The closer you get to awakening, the more likely you are to realize you don't know as much as you thought you did. The urge to know at all may get very stretchy and loopy, like a fishing net with lots of holes torn in it. Or a pocket that's had a seam ripper taken to it multiple times. After awakening (if you resist the temptation to think now you know everything), your hand may idly feel for the pocket and find it plumb gone, torn loose in the wind that blew away that person who used to think it was possible to know something about being.

Then you can stand in the presence of a tree, and sense how that's *you* over there. The tree can't, apparently, sense that you are just another one of it.

But then, you don't really know, do you?

17

The End of the Journey

There are two ways the spiritual journey can come to an end. Waking up is one of them. The other is to stop believing in the future. If you want to wake up, you need to see how important the future is to you. You've got to get real about this, so that all of your awareness can shift to the present.

When awareness is on the present, you're preparing the ground for awakening. When awareness is on the future, you're holding the prison gate shut.

The point of all spiritual effort is to discover the reality of what's already here. Not to become something different, but to see what you are *already*. When you wake up, you finally clearly see what's always been in plain sight.

This is not just a pretty way of saying something. Suppose it were the truth. What would that do to the idea that "maybe someday I'll wake up"? If you're already where you want to be, and you just don't know it, how does that affect the logic of the idea of a journey?

You can't be on a journey to someplace you already are. (Unless a journey inside your head counts for something.)

When you have that first awakening, the one where you realize you're in a kind of prison, where you see the problem isn't life so much as it's *you,* the most natural thing in the world is to look at where you are (suffering, reactive, mind-bound) and decide you want to be different. You'll need to grow in understanding, to evolve, let go of things, dismantle your ego. This will take time, you figure. The idea of the journey is born.

You may encounter the notion that you're "already there" but just don't know it. You may even say, *Yeah, I know I'm already free.* But the mind doesn't know what to do with that thought. You sure don't *feel* liberated.

You can see you aren't awake right now, and if you don't look to the possibility of some other time, what are you left with? The only thing the mind knows to do is say, *Well, maybe someday I'll wake up and actually* feel *free.* Your eggs have been put into the basket of some possible future.

The whole time, remember, the longed-for thing is right here. All the while your mind is trying to figure out how you can wake up, with your ego continuing to run the show—during every bit of the drama—the only real problem is that you can't see what's right in front of your face.

Somebody who knows he's in prison does not want to know there's no lock on the gate. Because if you're in prison, and you're the one that's holding the gate shut, then you have to face the truth that you're constantly free to leave.

It is not a comfortable place to be.

But once you acknowledge your part in the imprisonment, it then begins to be possible for something to actually change.

If you're waiting for one-of-these-days to deliver you to yourself, to render obvious your innate condition, you must see what comfort you're taking in the future.

You depend heavily on the idea that the future is a real thing. This is where hope is born. Otherwise, if you want to be awake but aren't now, what is there to do? Where are the eyes to fall but on tomorrow?

And what does *that* do but keep the illusion of time going?

Looking to a better possibility is what makes bearable the present imperfection. It's a way to avoid really looking at where you are now. Not just looking at it, but feeling. Yielding. Being absolutely truthful about what's going on. Belief in the future is an escape hatch.

But the future is the problem in the first place. Anything that nurtures belief in the reality of time puts you in your head. It puts you someplace besides presence. Telling yourself you aren't free puts attention the wrong place: someday.

You're taking consolation in something that exists only as a thought. There's no blood flowing through a thought. Time is an invention of the mind.

And it's only the mind that manages to invent despair out of this.

There *is* no prison. How can you suppose you're in it?

(See how convincing the mind is?)

Look at what happens. You don't feel free—you don't appear to be—so you tell yourself you aren't. Then you spend your life trying to become something you already are, instead of questioning how you get the impression of not being free. (The fact that your mind "understands" the idea that you already *are* the longed-for thing counts for nothing at all. As you are well aware, if you're truthful with yourself.)

If you tell yourself you're not free, then you miss seeing choice as it operates. You hide from yourself. Something in you says, *I'm doomed to suffer, to continue these patterns, until I become liberated.* This keeps you locked in a system that feels closed, when in fact it's not. Telling yourself you aren't free gives you a way to avoid looking at the myriad ways you keep your egoic self thriving. You neglect looking at how identified you are with things about yourself, at how automatically you react, how readily you resist, how you avoid your feelings. *Maybe I'll be awake someday,* you tell yourself, and you look away from the only thing that's real: the present. You avert your eyes from the very thing that would liberate you from the stream of thoughts trying to convince you they're *you.*

People can't stand to have their journey taken away from them. They need it to comfort themselves, because the place they seem to be at present doesn't feel very ecstatic or enlightened.

Ending the journey takes away escape routes, closes off the highways out of the burning city. Stay right there, in the exquisite discomfort of the reality of where you are. Find out how you delude yourself into thinking you're the sum total of your thoughts.

Find out who you really are.

If you can't look to the possibility of some other time, if you're left with nothing but this moment, and this moment feels bad, doesn't that make despair inevitable?

Only if you consult your mind. Only if you *think about* how you're not awake.

But if you step out of your mind into the present . . . if you let all of your awareness be with what-is, right now . . . despair over not being awake has no place to live.

Being perpetually stuck with now, with how you are *now,* is not a bad thing. The best thing that could ever happen to you is to have all of the gentle pressure of awareness brought right here.

When thinking starts up, notice it. When a thought comes (one like *I have to get better at staying present*), instead of indulging it, just look at it and say, *Oh, there's a thought.* You're back in presence.

The appearance of having come so far, of having tried so long and hard to wake up, is just a thought. Only in your head does it appear real. It has no objective reality.

The fact that it's real only in your mind isn't a comment on whether or not the thought is "true." It just means that it has no existence apart from your thinking about it. These apparent truths about your spiritual life literally come into being (like any belief) only when you start thinking. When you stop thinking, they dissolve as if they never existed. It's not as though the thoughts are still out there somewhere, being true, waiting for you to resume thinking them, noticing them, like neglected offspring.

The idea of a journey contributes to the seeker's particular brand of suffering, which comes (like most suffering) of not living in reality, of comparing *now* with something else. The seeker is one who wants but does not have, who tries but seldom succeeds. Who looks over the head of the present toward the desired future awakening. Who confuses mental understanding with visceral knowing.

Cut loose from the future. Pitch your tent in the burning city.

Anytime you notice yourself looking to the future for things getting better (not just about awakening, but about anything), feel how you take refuge there. See the *mind-made* relief of escaping present reality. Feel how good it is to have that idea of the future.

If you want to wake up, you must be willing to see how the effort to keep the egoic self alive is operating right now. To look in an unflinching, unresisting way.

See, we avoid that. We'd rather look to the future to rescue us from ourselves. We'd rather say, *Maybe someday I'll be without these issues.* The stuff we drag around from the past, the beliefs we're devoted to, our agendas, stories, emotional burdens, the things we identify with. We don't want to be with these things, to be truthful about the ways we nurture the impression that they're what we actually are. Because that would mean acknowledging our role in our own suffering.

You can have all the spiritual understanding in the world about how you "know none of that is who you really are." It's just a thought. Deeply, you *do* believe it's who you really are. Or you'd be awake already.

Be willing to see what consolation you take in *someday*. If you want to wake up, you have to see how uncomfortable you are with just being here, how readily you will escape it.

This moment is the (only) one in which there's some possibility of discovering your own complicity in this apparent imprisonment. If you must harbor any hope, locate it there. *If I stay with the present, I might eventually get a handle on my real problem.*

Declining to take refuge in some possible future lands you in a place where things can really start to happen. When you're willing to take your eyes off of maybe-someday, you start to see all the things you do, moment to moment, to keep your familiar self going.

If you weren't pretty constantly holding the prison gate shut, you'd be awake already.

This is the best terrible truth that could ever sink its teeth into you.

When you're intent on improving yourself, or you take solace in spiritual ideas (*I know my thoughts aren't real*), there's a setup for being out of alignment with reality. If you want things to really happen for you, it's essential that you bring your awareness in sync with what's real for you, now.

If you want to be different from what you are—if you want to wake up and stop being unconscious, reactive, resistant, identified—the tendency can be to deny your present condition.

This is because your focus is on your desired self, by contrast with your current real one. If on top of that, you use spiritual ideas to make it *okay* that you're unconscious (because you "aren't your limited self"), you have a recipe for a conflict that will keep you good and stuck. The conflict is between what-is and what you wish were so, or between what-is and the good spin you put on it. If you stay in this conflict, never facing yourself, you miss seeing how your ego functions in present-tense experience, where the recognition of choice-in-action—and the living possibility of change—can take place.

It's essential to be where you are. To not create that conflict. So something can actually change.

You're in a struggle between being-this-way and wanting-to-be-that-way. You don't want to be where you are (you want to be awake), so you avoid present reality—which is ironically the only place you can get insight that can ultimately free you. Instead, you resort to some spiritual idea about yourself, or the prospect of one day doing better. Neither of those things will help you. What they will do is keep you right where you are.

Trying to feel and act more evolved than you are puts your attention at an ever-growing distance from your ego mind, and that distance keeps the conflict going.

If you bring yourself to see how much resistance you're in, only then does it become possible to drop it. But if you deny it's happening (because you know it isn't very evolved to resist), then your attention is going not into acceptance but into avoidance.

Attention is a commodity of enormous value. Be judicious about what you do with it.

Look to see if you're in this kind of conflict between where you are and where you want to be; between reality and conceptual spirituality.

See yourself not as you wish to be, but as you really are. Then watch what happens.

Later on, if you wake up and look back over your history, you might think you can see what looks like the journey you took to get there. What you think you see, a series of significant moments, may or may not be what really woke you up. The mind will still enjoy thinking it can understand. Still, by then you'll be pretty comfortable with being unsure of things. It won't matter very much that you understand what led to the eventual breaking apart of illusion. Chances are, an awful lot of it took place below the mind's radar. And half of what you thought you knew about yourself at the time has turned out to be mental invention. But even if you think you can see something, a journey that led to awakening, it would be apparent only in retrospect. It would never have been visible ahead of time.

It's like Steve Jobs said in his commencement address to the 2005 graduating class of Stanford University. You may be able to connect the dots backward, but you just never could have done it in advance. Any way you look at it, forward or backward, the impression of a journey is still just a thing in the head.

It isn't for lack of understanding that you're still living life as your ego. It's because you aren't willing to go where you need to go.

Nobody and nothing can save you from the open-eyed tunneling into your interior. It's why your spiritual practice, your path, your teacher, can take you only so far. Nobody can go with you. But go you must.

You're on your own because your way of keeping your familiar self going isn't anybody else's way. Nobody but you occupies your present. Nobody but you can feel your ego thrive in this lived moment. Nobody but you got to be who you are, ticking the exact way you do.

Nobody but you can finally let the whole thing stop.

Here's where courage gets to be a blazing fire. Watching all of this play itself out happens most profitably in the very moments you're most vulnerable, when you've got the most at risk. When the last thing you want to admit to is that choice is at play.

Seeing the thinness of the invented self (and finally letting it blow apart) is not something that happens when you're sitting in a comfortable chair, out of the fray, calmly reflecting on your ego. It's something that happens when you're under siege.

Live in the present. Stay in feeling. See what happens when you keep awareness there. Notice when the mind wants to start up with its story, its objection. Watch what happens when emotions begin to brew, when beliefs insist their way into the scene.

When you stay with it, when you keep aware of the antics, at some moment a quiet voice may whisper, *Wait, I'm doing this deliberately.*

Then a pause, an electric realization: *I don't have to do this.*

These are the moments when the light goes on. Being with the messiness of what-is lets you see choice operating—not just the obvious, familiar kind of choice (to take this action, to react a certain way), but also the fundamental choice: to equate a thought with reality, to live as though you are your ego.

As though you are at the mercy of life.

These are the moments when you begin to feel the truth of what you've been told: that you are, in fact, free.

Notice: the sudden radical insight into living choice did not come from trying to change yourself. Trying to change would have distracted you from seeing the truth about yourself. The visceral discovery of choice came from the willingness to be where you really are. From watching the ego take on energy in an actual life experience.

Before liberation, you are free
but you live as though you are not.
After liberation, you are free
but you live as though you are.

There will, of course, be moments when you're aware of choice operating, yet cannot manage to take it into your hands. You watch yourself deliberately opt to hold on to your narrow sense of self, *as if you cannot help it.* You see yourself identifying, or you react emotionally or get busy spinning a story. Even so, you can stay aware as it goes on—if your courage holds. You can watch it all happen, observing how hard you work (and how much it hurts) to keep yourself going. To keep going the idea that you are not free.

Don't look away, no matter what.

Having a significant shift in awareness makes you able to see things you couldn't see before, because your perspective has shifted. Some block is gone. When one thing loosens up, others (dependent on it) are likely to soften as well. If you can now see choice operating where before you couldn't, choice will probably show itself more and more. It's as if a door has opened, and when you step through, you can see other doors (previously invisible) beyond that one. If you're noticeably more able to step outside of a thought and see it as such, you may find you're less inclined to buy into thoughts in the first place.

You may notice you're better equipped to be truthful with yourself, to be less resistant. Probably more of your egoic self will become transparent to awareness, simply because you're less prone to identify all you do and believe as being *you*. When your grip on what-you-know lessens, you're likely to find yourself increasingly comfortable with uncertainty and lack of control, and less inclined to strive for superficial security.

At times, you may experience periods of backsliding into the pull of patterns you thought you were done with. Don't waste energy on getting discouraged. Just stay with what's happening, without resistance, and keep aware. The long-established patterns of egoic response do not always readily dissolve just because you've seen through them. They may try again and again to reassert themselves. When this happens, just see it for what it is: the self, feeling threatened, naturally flares up as a device to keep alive. If you don't indulge the antics, but just step outside and watch them in motion, after a while they will lose steam. Eventually, like a child exhausted by a tantrum, they will quiet down.

Not every moment is devoted to keeping the familiar self alive. When you live in the present, with the readiness to see the truth, you'll have moments of calm. The steady willingness to see what-is calls attention not only to moments of suffering, but just as surely to the sweetly uncomplicated times when presence is felt to be a living thing. When life is just being life, and you feel yourself as simply a part of what-is.

Not a bunch of thoughts. Not an important individual. No experience at all of being in a prison.

More and more, if you fall out of love with the future, these moments will come.

Anytime you feel yourself come into present-moment awareness, *pay attention*. Notice how the whole world wants to stop here. Let it.

At such a moment, you might say something to yourself in recognition. Some small word that acknowledges, that says, *Look, see what's happening*. A simple thing like *This* or *Yes*. Like a greeting.

Oh (you could say), *it's* you.

Presence has come, like a blessed thing. You're paying homage. So plain. Simple.

Magnificent.

Allow yourself to linger here. Feel what it is to be in reality. If you died right now, it would be okay.

Don't wonder whether it will "last." (The wish for continuance is a thought.)

See how the idea of something lasting (or recurring) can make sense only in the thinking mind?

Something in you knows you are susceptible to another kind of existence.

As change occurs, as you come to experience freedom alive in your present awareness, you'll notice you no longer tap dance to every tune that once played in your head. Things that mattered a lot won't anymore. You won't be so identified with what you do, with your history. The tendency to resist unwelcome developments will hardly start up. You'll experience stretches of time when your mind is quiet.

And maybe you'll wonder less and less whether you'll ever wake up.

The Freedom of Being

18

Preparing the Ground

How does the longing to awaken express itself? The desire sits in the body, in the heart, and wants to take form. It might blossom into the idea of evolution, a destination, a journey.

But all of that assumes time exists.

There's another way the longing to awaken can take form. It's the idea of preparing the ground.

What is it to prepare the ground? It's to till the earth that is your self. To present to life a yielding surface, not an impenetrable shield. It's to do this right now, and again now. So that if the rain surprises you this moment, or this one, it will be taken in.

The focus is not on tomorrow, but on the present. When you're preparing the ground, you've forgotten about the idea of maybe-someday.

You are not in charge of whether the rain falls. On the long list of things that cannot be known or controlled is the matter of whether, or when, that final thing will happen to rinse the dust from your eyes.

But you *can* decline to score points for the other side. You can let go of rigidity. You can opt not to tighten against this moment, instead flooding it with presence.

Not to say you do this as a means to an end. Preparing the ground must be an end in itself. It's done for its own sweet sake.

The rest must take care of itself, if it will. If it will not, and you've been cultivating presence for its own sake, then you'll hardly notice whether awakening ever comes to stay.

Oddly, you may find that the closer you get to awakeness, the less obsessed with it you are. When the orientation to your life distills down to your orientation to *this moment*, when you're more truly content with life as it unfolds, you've come to where it's not so much on your mind, the question of whether you'll ever wake all the way up. Not because you've met with despair along the road to awakening, and have thrown up your hands. But because when you take your eyes from some possible future, and let them settle on where you are (now, now), then the idea of having someplace to go, some condition to attain, is seen to be just that—an idea. A thought. This moment is entirely captivating of attention. When you're less focused on doing better, and more accepting of the truth of where you are, you can fall out of love with the dream of tomorrow. How could there be someplace else to be but this, here?

The concept of future attainment becomes nonsensical once you really get that *this* is all that's real.

Isn't that what the whole thing's about?

What better way to prepare the ground than to be alive to the present? What could be a more fertile field for transformation?

This is something you really can do. Feeling yourself in the act of being makes you available to awakening like nothing you could dream of.

Who would awakening come to, if not one who's awake to this moment?

See how the question becomes silly, when this moment is all there is, ever? The question *will I ever wake up?* Laugh it off. Lift your face to the sky.

What if it were to rain?

The difference between trying to awaken and preparing the ground is the difference between strained mental/emotional effort and steady, unflinching presence. Trying to wake up is hard work. Wheel spinning, mostly. Hiding from yourself. It puts you in your head, where you scrutinize your every move, where you rain judgment on yourself, where you struggle to change yourself, and are forced to see you're back where you were before. It's because of all this that the spiritual journey is arduous, and exhausting, and largely unproductive.

Preparing the ground conjures a delightful calm, an alert receptivity, which is very different from a determined mission to transform yourself, to reach a goal. Let go all of that in favor of the simple, radical gesture of being *here*. Keep awareness on your interior. Feel what you feel, that original response to a thing. Feel life living itself through you. The gong reverberating deep in, each moment. Be *that*. Yield to the force of that, to whatever life delivers. Be conscious, unresisting, in devoted attendance on what's here, within you and without.

Preparing the ground is about what you allow to be primary, in your moment-to-moment existence. It's letting *attention* be front and center, always. There *is* something you can do, but it isn't a doing so much as a being. The thing you want, which is to be awake, is to be gotten to by being awake to this moment. The longed-for thing is attained by doing—by *being*—the longed-for thing. A person might want it to be more complicated than that. It isn't.

Preparing the ground is allowing as how you don't know (much of anything). It's declining to let what's happening stick to you.

It's about defending against nothing, about yielding. Letting in the sun and the rain, the wind and the hail. The scorching heat.

If attachment is happening, see it. If resistance is happening, see it. If identification is happening, see it. If fear, if grasping, if taking refuge in belief, see it. *Do not look away.*

Be soft, present. Ceaselessly look at what's happening right now to keep going the impression of there being a prison gate with a lock on it.

Do not go looking for an experience, some intensity or great moment of insight. Do not compare this moment with any other. The you that existed then is not the you that exists now. Every exhale, let the exhaling self cease to be. Feel the newly assembling presence come in on the new breath. Feel life give birth to itself again and again, in the ever-renewing awareness.

Be transparent, the moment passing through you and you through it. Feel yourself being the moment. If something is uncomfortable, open your arms to it. Don't grab onto it. It doesn't need to cling to you if you don't hold on to it.

Never think the content of the moment must be grand, or peaceful, or uplifting. What moment is not here? What *now* is not fit to be the one that brings the great blessing? Do you think washing your hands couldn't be it? Jacking up your car? Cleaning up broken glass? Hanging your head over a toilet?

How many moments do you suppose there will be in this day, in what remains of your life?

But *this* one: it's the one you have, the one you *are*. Tend it.

19

Loving Your Ego

There's more than one way to look at an ego. Your perspective on it is subject to change. (Remember, perspective is everything.)

How would you expect to experience the ego after awakening?

Do you *like* your ego?

What's likely is that the spiritual-seeker part of your mind thinks of the ego as a bad guy, but in fact you love it desperately.

If you wake up, neither of those impressions (villain, beloved) will hold water anymore. And you may be surprised to find that your ego didn't actually go away.

It's because you *want* to have an ego that you don't wake up. (Never mind what the spiritual-seeker part of yourself protests about wanting to destroy the ego. It hasn't convinced you so far, has it?)

Why would a person want to have an ego? Why is it so hard to stop living in thrall to it? Because something in you thinks that if the ego stopped running the show, you'd cease to be.

As much as you want to wake up, the idea of continuing to *be* trumps that longing. Day in and day out.

Running in the background is the assumption that the "death" of the ego (the end of identifying it as *you*) requires physical death, since there's a strong association between the inner (mental/emotional) self and its outer expression in the body, in observable life. It's hard to believe that the one could die without taking the other with it. So any threat to the familiar self feels like an existential threat.

No wonder such care is lavished on keeping the ego alive and well.

No wonder belief in an afterlife is so compelling.

It isn't the presence of the ego that's in the way of awakening. It's that you mistake it for who you are.

It's hard to imagine how the two things could coincide: continuing being, and ceasing to be attached to all you're used to defining as *you*. You invest your egoic self with a sense of reality, living as though this flimsy, insubstantial thing actually counts for something. It becomes an entrancing phenomenon. It's natural you'd be reluctant to walk away from it, in favor of something it's hard to imagine being (nothing—or everything).

The mind, which is the one trying to manage all of this, cannot imagine a mode of continuing-to-be besides the one you're accustomed to: the one that equates you with your ego. Try as you may, you cannot hope to undo this confusion via your mind, since it's the one mucking things up in the first place.

Stop trying to sort it out with your mind. The thing to do is to orient to your "self" differently from the way you've been doing it so far. To look from a different place. Not to have different *thoughts* about your self, but to observe your-self-at-play, in moments of actual life, in a way you may not have before. In order to look at your self, you have to step outside of it. Look not with the eyes of the ego, but with the eyes of presence.

So far, when you've been *thinking* about all of this, it's basically been the ego looking at itself in a mirror. Useless. (The mirror hangs inside the prison cell.)

You've got more than one looker at your disposal. This is key. When you are present with the moment, and aware of yourself "in" it, you can see things you don't ordinarily see, when you're just thinking about yourself.

The looker that is living presence is not afraid of its demise. It doesn't confuse itself with your ego. Yet it can *see,* can't it?

When you do this looking, it almost doesn't matter what you see. The significant thing is the looking itself. That perspective from which it's possible to know that you never were your ego.

The part of you that can do this seeing is lonely for its own company. It wants you to give up all the struggle and just be *that.*

Why can't I wake up? When you have a thought like this, realize that the awake presence within would never think to ask such a question. So the answer to the question is . . . to laugh at the question. *Silly ego: there it goes again, asking questions.* The thing to do is not to attempt to answer. The thing to do is to realize that the one asking the question is, in the first place, a fool. It isn't *you.*

The ego-mind, of course, being a curious creature (and ever in search of content), *wants* to think about these things. It imagines it can understand something outside of itself (using its puny light to illuminate beingness), but of course it is ill-equipped to do so. It can't help believing it's capable of seeing outside its windowless cell.

Consciousness does not ask, *Why can't I be free?* Consciousness *is* free. It is freedom itself. When a question like that arises, it's announcing itself as the production of the mind. Don't indulge it. Simply remember yourself. The next moment, as higher awareness flowers, the question will dissolve inside the flower.

What you need to do is figure out how *life* (the present moment, as you experience it) keeps you believing you are your ego, which is the sum total of your thoughts about yourself.

Lose the love affair with your psychological make-up, with your "problems." If you aren't ready to do this, then relax into the truth that you aren't ready to wake up. (Yes, sometimes it happens that a deeply attached person goes into terrible despair, or experiences a crushing blow to identity, and is forced into awakening. Not that you would wish devastation on yourself. In any case, you can't bring it about deliberately.)

When someone has a dark night of the soul and comes out the other side into awakening, she didn't "solve the problem" that made her want to die. What's happened is this: the self wanting to die (the one with the problem) ceased to feel real to her. She ceased to experience that person as being who she is. So what's necessary, this side of awakening, is to get your attention off of your "problems," and put it entirely on what sustains the self that's able to experience a *problem.*

Ask yourself this: how is it that someone could be in utter devastation, in that black night of the soul, and yet there turns out to be something *beyond* that? Something free, unburdened—not only of the so-called problem, but of the potential for any problem at all?

It's right there that you must put your attention, as you're living moment to moment. Keep yourself on that line—the one dividing the place where a problem can exist, from the place where it cannot. If you focus on a problem *as though it really is a problem,* you're keeping going the impression that you are your egoic self.

Ask yourself unceasingly, *What's going on this moment that's keeping going the impression that I am my ego?*

If you aren't willing to live there, then stop saying you want to wake up. Give yourself a break.

If you *are* willing, if you want this thing that much, live on that line.

Discover how you feed your limited self. Look at the structure that holds up the whole thing. How do you manage to keep believing your apparent self matters? What belief systems do you cling to? What do you most deeply identify with? What have you not been willing to look at, to let go of? What do you lie to yourself about? Where do you throw up a smoke screen of spiritual understanding as something to hide behind?

Something in you, probably beneath conscious noticing, is convinced that you benefit from identification with certain things about yourself. It thinks that staying attached to particular beliefs does you some kind of good. These are the things you need to be willing to look directly at. They have everything to do with why the mind-made self feels like who you actually are. What do you get out of clinging to the sense of self you carry everywhere you go? (If you didn't get something out of it, you wouldn't do it.)

As Sogyal Rinpoche puts it:

> [The ego's] greatest triumph is to inveigle us into believing its best interests are our best interests, and even into identifying our very survival with its own. This is a savage irony, considering that ego and its grasping are at the root of all our suffering. Yet ego is so convincing, and we have been its dupe for so long, that the thought that we might ever become egoless terrifies us. To be egoless, ego whispers to us, is to lose all the rich romance of being human.

It can be maddening to think you understand how the ego works, yet it continues to drive your every move. It's because there are things you haven't looked at, from the clear point of view *outside* the limited self. Find out why you hold on to the egoic identity. If you think of yourself as a victim, as someone who's chronically ill, as a survivor, a renunciant, then something deep in can suppose that the end of this identification would rob you of a sense of self.

You hold beliefs of all kinds. If someone asks what you think about thus-and-so, you'll almost always have a ready viewpoint, perhaps one you came to long ago. Your ideas about what's *true* (for that is what a belief is) constitute a significant part of who you are.

Ask yourself who you'd be without any beliefs at all. When you wake up, these cherished ideas will cease to feel important, since their primary function is to give you a "you." The egoic self does not readily turn away from the things it believes to be true. Yet any belief system (even a spiritual one that seems to be helping you) is limiting. Beliefs talk to the mind, not to presence. They intervene between awareness and reality. They attempt to interpret reality, putting you at a distance from it.

You don't necessarily need to examine systematically every single thing about your ego (since when some parts self-destruct, others will fall with them, no longer able to sustain themselves). But you must be *willing* to look at anything. There can be no sacred cows.

What do you suppose is the cost of liberation? Where is the limit to what you're willing to face?

In the usual way of looking at the mind, you see a self producing thoughts. That's clear. What's not so obvious is that the *thinker* (that is, the appearance of a you) is really just another one of the thoughts. An elaborate thought, to be sure, but invented just as sure as the thoughts are invented. You think yourself up (over and over again) and then the self you thought up thinks thoughts. That is what becomes very clear when you've awakened: that your mind has been inventing a self your entire life.

The thought and the thinker-self that thinks it up are both things. Like a door is a thing, or a cricket, or a shoe. The thinker-self looks like a more objectively "real" thing than the familiar sort of thought. But in truth, the self, as you perceive it, is just an integrated mental production that's incredibly complex.

When people try to imagine what it would be like to be awake, they often suppose that upon awakening, they'll be the same sort of being, only one filled with joy and equanimity. They don't realize that the person they think they are (including the one trying to figure out how to awaken) is just as much made up as the thoughts made up by the person they think they are. Which is to say, the thinker and the thought belong to the same order of reality. Manufactured.

What's impossible to imagine, this side of awakening, is that "you" will not be here anymore. That self will have lost the ability to believe in itself as a stable entity. Yes, joy and equanimity will abound; but they won't be "yours."

It appears that the thinker is on some other plane than the thoughts, that the thinker has an existence independent of the mental activity that gives it life. People who want to stop suffering *really* want to believe in this model, because they want to know what it feels like to be themselves *sans* pain.

It's natural to want to dignify the made-up self. It has, after all, a dignified history, and a load of memories, with scars and photographs to show for it. But when waking-up happens, that person with the important string of events to its credit turns out to be very much like the dream you had last night. Just about that worthy of note. Imagine, and after a lifetime of thinking you were so important, you and your issues and your longing and points of view. Imagine losing interest in yourself, but that's what happens.

You may suppose that you're getting pretty good at not dignifying your thoughts. But you might still be really in love with your thinker. Very likely you are. The reason it's a pretty good bet is that probably you have trouble believing your thinker is really just a complicated thought: that you have, in fact, made it up.

When you wake up, your ego doesn't exactly disappear. It's just that you've stopped thinking it's *you*. In its unaccessorized version (detached from its defining features), an ego can be seen to still exist, even to be *necessary*. It's adopted anytime you function on the level of form. A modest version of ego is needed in order to experience that you have a physical manifestation, to notice a sensory impression, to figure something out, to take action, interact with others, have fun, name a phenomenon, tell a story. It's necessary to experience a self in order to do any of the things a self does. However, this basic engagement with the physical world, with ordinary human life, in no way requires you to believe that you *are* your history or the roles you play or your opinions.

In formless awakened consciousness—awareness aware only of itself—you can be both conscious and conscious of nothing. Not even conscious of being a "somebody"-who-is-aware. If nudged by circumstance to remember yourself, to revisit your somebody-ness (the telephone rings, or someone walks into the room and says your name), you can readily slide back into self-ness and recall that you go with that name, that you are physical, and in a certain place, with something happening. But none of that is inevitable, in the default mode. All of that "coming back into yourself" involves stepping back into the role-playing ego, the pretense that we all routinely adopt in order to live our lives, do our jobs, have relationships, talk on the phone. But it can happen without *identifying* with any of it—if you're able to remember (viscerally) that you aren't your ego.

What would it be like to have your same personality, preferences, life conditions, and recollected experience without believing any of it is what you are? To do all you do without being attached to the outcome of any effort?

When you're watching yourself live, see if you can distinguish the facts-as-facts from the angst-laden ones. It's possible to have a chronic illness without *being* person-with-illness. It's possible to have been emotionally abandoned in childhood without *being* "someone with abandonment issues." You can run a business without experiencing a downturn as threatening to *you*.

It's like being an actor in a play. All the while you're dressed like a certain character, saying lines and doing things and gesturing, you never suppose you actually *are* that person. You enjoy the pretense of getting to "be" somebody. But you have no trouble dropping the pretense, and never for one instant do you confuse it with reality.

If you believe you are your limited-person egoic self, then for all practical purposes, that is what you are. Once you know it's just a role (*really* know it, not just in your spiritual mind), then it's not a problem anymore to wear the costume.

Don't bother trying to convince yourself you aren't really your ego. It's a total waste of time, a good way to stay stuck (because it's all happening inside the mind).

A productive alternative to that mind-talk is to notice, in actual present-tense moments of life, anytime you feel an assault on your sense of self. Noticing threatening episodes is a good way to identify the things that sustain your egoic self—the parts of you that you're reluctant to let go of, because they feel so essential to who you are.

Here's where living in *feeling* supports your longing for freedom, where awareness of your inner reality prepares the ground for awakening. Experiencing the moment at the feeling level keeps you in the present, and it may reveal (if you look) the outlines of some feature of your familiar self. As much as you can, stay with the primary response to something, rather than moving into the mind (justifying, judging, denying) and distorting the original feeling. Staying with the feeling may help you sense threat. When danger is perceived by who you appear to be, it's as if a raw nerve has been touched. Doubtless it's painful to linger there, and it asks a certain courage. But if you want to wake up, the discomfort may point to a prime suspect in the undercover ego operation. Since virtually all the effort of ego maintenance goes on below the level of conscious awareness, becoming more attuned to the present-moment feeling state has the power to expose the infrastructure of the familiar self.

Your attention may be alerted by a loss of control, guilt, the fear of exposure, or feeling misunderstood. Threat may take the form of feeling hurt or criticized, being outdone, revealed to be wrong or inadequate. There may be a challenge to a deeply held belief, or to something you take pride in. Maybe you perceive someone not taking you seriously, not sufficiently respecting your expertise or your background.

Awakened presence doesn't need to protect or defend itself. Any experience of threat (apart from a literal one to your physical well-being) is a reliable indicator that the ego is under siege.

Forget looking at your history, at patterns you've observed in the past. Looking at your general tendencies from afar is no substitute for feeling the bite of a real-life moment. What do you actually feel now? What's at risk here?

The idea is to learn to recognize your own signs of being under siege, to *feel* them taking place, to recognize them as early as possible. When you sense threat, although what's primary is the immediate discomfort, you're likely to hurry past that (at least initially) to the familiar pattern of defense. Because of the ego's efficient mechanism of self-protection (which you've perfected over decades), the earliest detection of an assault on the ego may be *not* the feeling of threat, but rather the defensive posture that comes in response to it. The repeated practicing of self-defense has made it function automatically and with breathtaking speed.

Well before you open your mouth or take action, a process is under way to protect you from feeling bad about yourself. You rely on thought patterns like *He's just being a jerk,* or *It isn't my fault the thing happened,* or *I'll do better next time.* This self-talk is like a safety net that appears whenever the occasion calls for it. The bad feeling (the primary response you try to avoid) may call attention—if you're willing to look—to a key feature of your identity, something you cling to like a life raft.

These quickly erected walls of defense must be allowed to topple like dominoes, so you can feel—and stay with—the sensation of threat. So you can know what is experiencing harm, and see the moment for what it is: an ax taken to a pillar of your ego structure. You need to be able to say to yourself, *Wow, I feel under attack here.* Allow the feeling of vulnerability.

See how fast you want to go into protect mode. Look how hard you work to keep yourself intact, how vigilant you are.

Whether you're used to reacting to threat-to-self in a cerebral way or you move quickly to an emotional reaction, you'll need to grow more attuned to that very early *feeling* response—the thing that happened *before* the mind got in on the act, prior to the furious heat of emotion. It takes courage to do this. There may be a fierce resistance to allowing the feeling. The more energetic this resistance, the more doggedly you insist on self-protection, the more certain you can be that there's a wild animal in your ego closet.

Note that none of this is about an *outer* response (though growing self-attunement will surely moderate behavior). It has entirely to do with the profoundly private response on your mental and emotional interior, in the secret rooms where the work of ego maintenance goes on.

Note, too, that this self-observation must go on without regard for whether you're "in the wrong." It's not about whether you "had it coming" (although if you know you're in the wrong, you'll doubtless be more reluctant to acknowledge the primary feeling).

The lifelong mechanisms of self-repair busy themselves with trying to sort out who's at fault, as if that's critically important. (It may be, but only to the ego.) They look for ways to put the blame anyplace but within. But this isn't about sorting out who or what is to blame. The question of responsibility or causality is very much beside the point here.

The ego dislikes that immensely.

You may find it illuminating to reflect on the kinds of situations where you tend to feel on shaky ground, wanting to hide or counterattack. See what you typically do, privately, to rise to your defense: stories you tell yourself (about other people, about your own limitations, your difficult history), internal name-calling, consolation or other mental escape routes, a promise to do better in the future, or to avoid a similar unwelcome situation. This reflection may help you notice the next time the self-defense mechanism starts up.

Everywhere you go, you carry your self with you. It's like a mind-made portable home that you live in. You feel secure in it (which seems to justify the terrible weight of the whole thing). There's a kind of comfort—*even if a lot of what you carry is painful*.

As your familiar self becomes less of a burden, and your life moves along with greater ease, you may notice you're no longer so hell-bent on "dismantling your ego." This is because your ego no longer seems to be who you are, in the convincing way it did before. Once you've stopped believing in it, there's no more need to vanquish it.

After you wake up, and all you've identified with has ceased to enchant you, you continue to experience "home" everywhere you go. But not because you're hauling a recognizable self from situation to situation. It's because you experience all-that-is as "you." So *everywhere* feels like home. There's nothing artificial to carry any longer. The need for security is gone.

There's no more prison cell. Everywhere you look, as far as the eye can see, just *home*.

20

Who Are You?

How would you complete this sentence?

I am ...

What comes to you? *I am ...* what? *I am a ...* what? *I am a person who ...* what? Sit in the feeling of that, a statement or two about yourself. See how such a statement names a feature, or a thing you do, or value.

I am a teacher.
I am depressed.
I am an immigrant.
I am a retiree.
I am a liberal.
I am afraid.

The details are not at all important. You could trade the end of your sentence with the end of somebody else's. Nothing significant would change.

See how the ego-mind warms to that idea.

What's important to focus on is that something—anything at all—follows that first thing: *I am.*

Sit in the feeling of one of your self-definitions. See the parts of the expression. There is a person here, and this person has this characteristic. Does this kind of thing.

Take your time.

●

Now remove whatever follows the word *am*. Let the end of the sentence float away on the breeze of forgetting, just for a moment, who you seem to be.

Sit in *I am*. Just that. Feel your way into the vast stillness at the center of all you are.

Notice that you be.

Sit for a long time. Sit until you've forgotten to notice how much time has gone by.

●

What is that, to be? Unadorned being, without quality or activity? Without history or desire? What is it to sense you are here, aware, but . . . nothing else at all? Or, nothing else that matters enough to find its way into awareness. Into some definition of a self.

After a time, even the *I* is felt to dissolve. All is *am*. Being. Being feeling itself be.

This is the primary reality. This is not a fancy experience, a thing extracted from substantial reality. It's not what you're left with when you forget yourself. It's where you arrive when you remember yourself. For

> . . . the end of all our exploring
> Will be to arrive where we started
> And know the place for the first time.

All the rest is ornament.

Do you see what's being said here? Your entire sense of yourself is artificial. Like plastic, like some suffocating synthetic fabric that cannot breathe. Every blessed thing you think about who you are. It's all a thought that has convinced you of its reality.

This is why when you awaken, none of it matters anymore. It's why you cannot be hurt. Why you don't fear. What can hurt formless being?

It is said God made the manifest world. That's impressive: something from nothing. But what could be more magnificent than pure formless being? This is what you are. This is why when you awaken, the sense is that you have come to know God.

As your very self. Not the self with qualities or memory or agenda. Yet in your very body, it is felt. In your deteriorating, rejoicing body, the vast everything recognizes its presence. And there is delight.

This is why at the end of each day of creation, the made thing was seen and pronounced *good.* Goodness recognized itself. The formless acknowledged its own presence in form. The fact that something was there, instead of nothing, meant that delight itself could take form.

The fact that a human being can sense the presence of all-that-is within his very self means that delight can be both manifest and boundless.

Why, then, would sorrow overtake you? How deep can forgetfulness go? On the surface of a life, sorrow plays, and beside it, longing. But when the stillness comes, and the *I-am* is allowed its breathing space, how can longing get a toehold? There is no one there to want. There is no lack.

Something in you does not wish for more than its own company. It is not dissatisfied. (What spectacular understatement.)

Let all that you think you are collapse like a marionette with its strings gone slack, and see what's left.

Take all your wanting, all your restless maneuvering, the entire terrible weight and noise of it. Put it in a box and tape it shut. Load the box onto a truck driving away from you and never coming back.

There is something left, isn't there? You are still here. You can feel yourself being.

Welcome home.

21

The Final Chapter

Some people devoted to waking up are excruciatingly self-aware. Fascinated bystanders to their own dissolution, they've watched the whole thing going on, for years maybe, observing themselves falling apart bit by bit. By the time they come around to hanging on by a thread, they are watching with a very careful eye. They surely know better than to think about what's going on, but it happens anyway. *How much longer is it going to take? Will it ever happen?* It can become a torture.

It never stops being the case that if you'll just stop thinking—if you'll put your attention on attention—the impression of discomfort will go away.

Say you begin to get your wish (maybe it's already happening), slipping more and more into that other awareness, the one where there are no problems. Only, as you leave yourself behind, little by little, you are sometimes unnerved. It's not so comfortable. That impression of the encroaching void. Hardly recognizing yourself. Maybe, too, the maddening push-pull, the familiar self acting up, trying to call attention to itself, protesting that you would miss it (maybe even die) if you were to fall out of love with it.

This is the part of awakening about which there are no bliss-ful fantasies. Where you feel yourself falling apart, and—no lon-ger knowing who you are, in any reliable way—you become scared.

Not everyone goes through this. The ease or dis-ease of the transition could have something to do with parts of the ego-self still seeming real, even as others are transparent. So, when the big shift starts to happen, those see-through aspects of a person sort of drag along the other ones, which follow reluctantly, like clattering cans behind the car of newlyweds, making a ruckus and stirring up dust.

Those parts do not go gladly into their own dissolution. Though go they will, if you can manage not to take them too seriously—which means, if you can keep remembering they aren't *you*. Just let them pitch their fit, even as you watch from a little bit of a distance. Keep that other presence steadily in the picture, so the apparent reality of the ruckus-maker isn't indulged.

Time is trying to take itself apart in your awareness. The per-son with memory and ambition and traces of past wounds does not welcome this. When the noise and foul odor come, be still. Just be still. Let it be. Find that presence within that knows only being. You can find your way to this, always. Don't invest effort in trying to stop the commotion, resolve conflicting forces, or even understand what's going on.

Just remember yourself.

What you are is so vast, so without quality or limit, that it can comfortably hold all that's troubling you. It all must play itself out. Before many more days have gone by, you'll look back and smile. You'll see how the discomfort spent itself, how need-less it was to be troubled.

You are a sopping towel that life is wringing out. Soon you'll be hung to dry. You will dance in the wind and the sun. The rain will come and soak you, but you won't be burdened by the weight of it. You'll just take it. Then the sun will come again.

But now, while you're trying to let go of yourself, trying to simultaneously hold on to and release useless appendages, decorations, encumbrances (like an identity, like the illusion of security, like any form at all of taking yourself seriously)—now, when torment comes, remember that you don't *have* to be in torment. Something in you has summoned it, and something else in you can open the window and let the old world suck it back out, where it belongs.

You are no longer of the old world.

The mind groans, *How can I know this? What if I am?*

It's just a thought.

At some point, you're no longer of the old world. You get to where you can't go back. You wouldn't know how. If I said "Drop this thing, forget it, go back and be your old self," you wouldn't know how. You wouldn't be able to do it, to pretend it matters, in the old familiar way. You're done with it. Now what's happening is that you're needing to give it the time it must take to be done with you. When you have ceased to let it get you, it will stop trying.

There's nothing to do but go forward.

When you feel searing pain, stand for it. Find in its heat the place that's empty, still, cool. Do you think your torment is of interest to the tree? the cloud? the pieces of wood that hold up the roof? But don't you see there's something *in you too* that's like this—that cannot be bothered with the little ups and downs? Find that. Be there. Know that *this* is what you are. It's waiting for you to fall into its embrace. It's waiting for you to cease to believe in the things you've invented.

When the burning pain comes, ask what of it has actual existence. What of it was born in your mind? What your mind makes of you is a mirage. Rest from it. You don't have to do this. Something in you thinks the pain-causer has a life of its own. See that you think this. It isn't so.

What do you think life will look like after this is all over? What about when it pitches you what once would have looked like a lousy ball? What will that be like, do you think? How will you stand in the presence of that? How will you hold the space in which it exists, in which the thing will play itself out? What will it feel like to have the wind of anything at all blow gently through you?

Hold this awareness now, in these times of the kicking and screaming. See how you can get bigger, how you can go beyond your body, your identity, to feel the pulsing world in which it's all taking place. Love has brought you this far. Love will take you all the way. With poignancy, you will look back at these days when you couldn't imagine anything beyond this knotted up ball of string.

Let it relax itself apart. The world is a big windy place.

Epilogue

O joy! that in our embers
Is something that doth live,
That nature yet remembers
What was so fugitive!

—WILLIAM WORDSWORTH

At the place where two things approach one another—the life of freedom and the life of longing for it—it's as if you're moving slowly toward your image in a mirror, palms facing out, about to make living contact with the other thing you are.

But your hands come to rest on this hard surface.

Going all the way may give you pause. Sometimes a person will say, *I'm not sure I want to lose myself.* Liberation looks like extinction, like dissolution.

If you love this world, if you love your life, it can be hard to imagine existence without there being a *somebody* to taste the sweetness. How can there be deliciousness without a tongue—without a separate self? Doesn't there need to be a finger to put to the honey, to lift the thick, glistening drop to the lips? If the finger dissolves into nothingness, if the sense of self goes completely away, then how can delight be experienced? How can love happen?

Once, a woman longing for freedom expressed this simultaneous reluctance. She loves the natural world, revels in the smell and the feel of it: wing and leaf, lavender and earthworm, wind and water, rock and bone. She savors it all, even predation and decay. She gets up close so she can brush up against it, roll in it practically, the way a dog will slather itself in something fragrant to a canine nose. She fills her worshipping hands with it, carries it to her altar. She makes it into poetry, so others can get the scent and texture of the world—so they can tell one yellow apart from another, can witness the moods of sun and sky, the outline and arc of every flying creature. She is scientist as much as poet. Nothing to her is ugly or unfortunate, nothing unworthy of song.

Just as vividly can this woman feel the release into freedom. In moments when she sees herself clinging to resentment, to expectation, and then lets it go, she can taste liberation as if she were the ruby-throated hummingbird, its tongue slipping through the slender black beak, the desperate quick darting into deliciousness. She knows the radical relief of the fleeting loss of self, the one that feels trapped and fearful and grim.

But the other: what about the self that rejoices in the physical world? Will she lose that too, if she wakes up?

And what about love, the human kind? The love of one person for another? The aching love for God? Will all of it dissolve into emptiness?

She senses the approach to the edge, the point beyond which there is no restoration to the familiar, and she hesitates.

What can I say to her? That the bird she so loves will no longer be *other*, a thing out there for her to observe from a distance? That she will not miss being moved to tears at the way its wing color changes according to its tilt toward or away from the sun? How can I help her to see she will *become* the bird, the sunlight, the blue-then-green of the wing? That when her familiar sense of self finally altogether dissolves—when she approaches the edge of the known and keeps going—she will *be* the exquisite world. Be the honey, the wind, the brook, the shape of the hillside, the bleaching bones.

When you cease to be separate from what you love, love hasn't ceased to be. Love revels in its own presence, without regard for where "you" are in it. The particulars of form have become incidental. When lover and beloved are no longer distinct, love feels itself moving everywhere, always.

There doesn't need to be a separate perceiving self—a hungry, reaching, exclaiming self—in order for celebration and delight to come into being.

Presence *recognizes itself* in the living awareness of a bodied intelligent animal. It recognizes itself everywhere it looks. Everything that happens is love assuming form, and dissolving back out of it.

The manifest world—you, all you experience, all you love— is emptiness embodied. Doesn't the formless assume form in order that it might have a way to rejoice in itself?

In the formless silence of a human heart—before idea, before preference or desire or personality—there is a stillness where knowing is. There's nothing for knowing to hold on to. Yet knowing *is* . . . and it *feels* itself. It experiences itself in all that is. It is without time, without word, without identity. Yet it lives.

What you have known to be within yourself is discovered to be the essence of all-that-is. You look into the eyes of another, and what do you see there but yourself. You look at a tree, and there you are. How can there be anything *but* love?

Do you love God then? You no longer have the experience of reaching for that which you are not separate from.

What is it to be bodied, mortal, and also to be emptiness? To live a life, and yet not be at the mercy of life? Here is the magnificence: to be all-that-is, and within that, to be father, daughter, mate, patient, flute-maker, trucker.

What is the incarnation, if not this? Here, yet not afraid. Not wanting, or struggling. Outside the push and pull of time. Empty, and even so, aware. Alive, swimming in tenderness.

What is it to sense the entire sky within your chest? To wander in the dark infinity and not feel the need to search for your "self"? What is it to be a person, and to be free?

Find out.

Step into freedom and move from there, ever after knowing what you are.

Afterword

A Postscript to
When Fear Falls Away

There are two realizations. The first is when you are realized—
when you become real. The truth of what you deeply are is
realized. Illusion is abandoned, and you experience being one
with all that is, with reality.

The second is when you *realize* what has taken place. When
you understand what it is, the "it" that has come about. The two
realizations are often separated, sometimes by years.

Some who have the first realization (the one that counts)
never arrive at the second one. They know they are different (from what they were, from other people), but they never
know why—what it is about themselves. They never stumble
onto a book, or a person, who's able to explain them to themselves.

There are some for whom the two realizations are a single
moment, the upheaval and the *fathoming* being all of a piece.
Prior knowledge of the phenomenon has perhaps prepared
them for this simultaneity. They watch it happen, and know
what they are seeing. They may have been seeking.

For some, there is no discernible moment of transformation. They don't feel it when it happens. The radical shift occurs quietly, below the radar. They will never be able to point back to a moment and declare, *That is when the old way ended.* All they can say is, at some point they realized that things had changed. The noticing dawned only gradually.

●

How is it that we come to know anything we know about ourselves? How does the recognition arrive, the moment of revelation? Something you hadn't known about yourself has revealed itself. You may be a little startled by the discovery. Perhaps the thing was so deep-in that you hadn't sensed it before. Or maybe something fundamental has changed, and you're just now realizing it.

Sometimes a bone breaks in such a way that the sharp edge ruptures the skin, and for the first time in your life you are seeing a part of yourself you've never seen before (nor expected to). Some terrible injury tears you open, giving your eyes sudden and horrible access to a feature of your interior: the meat of a muscle, the slippery tissue of a pulsing organ.

Setting aside the certain pain and fright of such a moment, there's something of a simple cognitive shock involved, the mind registering, *I didn't know this about myself before.*

It'd be like seeing, for the first time in your life, your image in a mirror. *Huh,* you'd say. *Will you look at that.*

●

I didn't write about it at the time, when I might naturally have. I never attempted to describe the life-altering moment of *getting it*—of understanding the nature of the change that had taken place almost a year before.

The oh-my-God moment.

At the time the understanding dawned, I was too overwhelmed to attempt to articulate it. Everything in me was going into simply processing what I'd seen.

Later, assembling eighteen months' worth of writing into a book, I was well aware that a key piece of the story was missing. I let it be.

●

It was July. My partner and I were in Maine. We were sitting on the shore near the cabin we'd rented for the week. We had a book with us, Franklin Merrell-Wolff's *Pathways Through to Space*.

I can find the place in that book. I can put my finger to the passage I was reading aloud, the words I'd just said into the salt air of a warm day, when my companion said the thing he said, and then I thought the thing I thought. Suddenly I knew. *Knew,* like a crack of thunder inside my body. Nearly a year after the fact, I got what had happened to me the previous August.

He had just applied to the two of us something said in the book. Inherent in his observation was an assumption that we had something in common. I saw with a shock that it may be true of him, but *it was no longer true of me*. I had left behind the condition of the vast part of humanity.

I said nothing of what I'd seen. I recall vividly how utterly still I became, the stunned disconnect between what was going on in awareness and whatever I was saying, whatever my eyes must have been seeing: his face, the ocean, the clouds, the book splayed on my knees. I remember struggling to conceal that something was going on, to compose my face in such a way— some bland, featureless way—that wouldn't call attention to me, that wouldn't cause him to say, *What? What is it?* I wished I could disappear. Taking in the enormity was requiring every available resource.

We must have gone on reading. I must have lowered my eyes back to the page, my mouth mechanically producing the words in the next sentence, and the next. But everything in me was laser-focused on what I had just seen.

It's enlightenment. That's what's happened.

Merrell-Wolff had laid out an elaborate picture of the world of consciousness, including his delineation of the levels ("seas") of humanity.

At the top is the Grand Sea of Infinite Consciousness, inexhaustible and without bounds. This is the seeming Emptiness that actually is the Fullness of the SELF—Pure Divinity, the Base of all else and the Final Resolution of all things. The next is the plane of Cosmic and Transcendent Consciousness. Here the One is also a Brotherhood. Likewise, permanence stands united with evolution. Below there is a gulf, not easy to cross; a gulf that mankind, in its folly, has widened while the Few, dedicated through Love to that mankind, strive ceaselessly to bridge the chasm. *The third sea is the level of egoistic, or subject-object, consciousness in its highest state of development, the genuine upper-class of egoistic humanity. Here is the consciousness of those who move on the higher levels of love and intellect, but still within the limits of subject-object consciousness. These form the real "Chosen Race." Without them, the gulf would be impassable for the great human mass, and then, ultimately, all would sink down and out through the sluggish sea of ignorance. Of the human whole only a handful, relatively, abides in the third sea, yet they are the immediate sustainers of all civilizations, the* real *burden-bearers of this outer life. From among them also come the recruits that, now and then, succeed in crossing the gulf.* The fourth sea is of narrow limits, but heavily crowded with a large proportion of humanity. These are the quasi-intellectual, the semi-cultured, the mass that has become conceited with a little knowledge and does not know the saving humility of much knowledge. On this level are the senseless disputations fraught with emotion and passion. This is where the surgings arise that cause the turmoil of nations and classes. Yet there is some Light here, and the energy generated by Desire, the latter, to be sure, untrained and poorly directed, but still affording a force that eventually may be harnessed and guided. There still remains much hope for these despite their great folly. The fifth sea, shallow and very constricted, is densely crowded with the greatest mass of all. These are the sodden ones, drugged from drinking the final dregs of passion, those who bear little of the burden, but who are themselves the great burden. This sea is murky with the stirred-up mud of the depths, so there is only a dim twilight of the self-conscious light here. Yet there is a degree of self-consciousness, and so this lower realm does stand above the animal, even though sinking, in many respects, deep into the animal consciousness, and, by this illicit union, producing something lower than the animal. [*italics mine*]

"So you and I must be in the third sea," my partner reflected aloud. Meaning that we occupied Merrell-Wolff's "upper-class of egoistic humanity . . . still within the limits of subject-object consciousness."

Yes, I thought. *I have been there.* That condition was familiar . . . and yet now, I saw . . . haltingly . . . *it was a thing of the past.*

For me.

"From among them also come the recruits that, now and then, succeed in crossing the gulf."

It was Merrell-Wolff who held up the mirror to my face.

Aftershock upon aftershock now, in the days following. *How could I not have understood?* So much finally made sense. All the months of seeing how every single thing about myself was changed, gone, undone. Now it was beginning to add up.

Why had it taken so long for me to get it?

I had never in my wildest dreams supposed that *that* could happen. Who among even the most ardent of spiritual seekers ever supposes that the longed-for thing—the absolute relief from suffering—could rain its blessings upon her?

Yet even as I'd watched it all come alive (the absence of fear, reactivity, need, desire, negativity; the end of being caught up in my history, of wanting to control or change other people; the weirdly quiet mind); even as my entire awareness had become saturated in ceaseless joy and ease; even as I'd staggered around for months in the condition, thoroughly and unmistakably altered—even so, I did not understand that this was *That*. That what had happened was the ultimate thing.

●

Long after the fact, I see I was fortunate to not understand, for a time, what was going on. (Not that I tried very hard, the experience itself being what mattered, not having a name for it.)

Having no mental framework meant I was able to simply *live* it: to be in the unfolding of this miraculous thing, without an intervening lens to interpret by. There was nothing in my head to distract from pure experience. Unburdened by ideas, I was simply immersed.

Sometimes when a woman gives birth to a baby whose gender she didn't know ahead of time, she'll choose to bond with it for some minutes before discovering the features that will define its identity ever after. The baby is simply, for a time, beloved being. It was like that, for me, for eleven months. Having no explanation, nor much of a drive to find one, I was free to revel, to look around at the strange and wonderful terrain, both entirely new and somehow utterly familiar.

Not that finally having a name diminished my delight. If anything, it enhanced it—not (as one might suppose) because now I could somehow feel more joy than I already did, or because I could imagine I had "achieved" something great (nothing had been "done" by "me"). No, it was that finally having a conceptual framework enabled me to do that uniquely human thing: to *understand*. My thinker-self was now able to align with the other awareness, the one that knew only boundlessness, that couldn't feel any other way but joyful.

Acknowledgments

I extend my heartfelt thanks to the many people who encouraged me to write this book. I'm filled with appreciation for everyone who's organized a teaching event, with special thanks to Paloma Hill. Brand new at this, Paloma put heart and soul into inventing the wheel, and (with her band of merry collaborators) rolled it up and down Northern California, bringing me into the presence of so many wonderful people, not to mention those magnificent trees.

My love and gratitude to my dear friend Mary Mauzey, whose encouragement and support are as big as the sky.

Many thanks to Peter Klein for the beautiful website, and for his generosity and love through every chapter. To Paul Kaufman, for his friendship and for turning his life inside out. To Anne Chandler and Lou White for shared laughs and brimming emptiness, for the enduring pleasure of their company.

I am grateful to Michael Walsh for discerning the difference between feeling and emotion, and for much else besides.

Abundant gratitude to Gary Leon Hill for helping me come to the point, and for the depth of appreciation; to Suzanne Kingsbury for early guidance; and to Jan Johnson for her publishing wisdom and her humanity.

Finally, to all those who long to know the truth, to discover the unwoundable joy within—I am constantly moved by your courage and openness, your willingness to keep letting go. Being in your presence is pure joy.

References

Book Epigraph

T. S. Eliot, "Little Gidding," in *T. S. Eliot: Collected Poems 1909–1962* (Harcourt, Brace & World, 1930).

Introduction

Robert Browning, "Andrea del Sarto," in *Selected Poems of Robert Browning* (Appleton-Century-Crofts, 2011).

Wallace Stevens, "The Poems of Our Climate," in *The Collected Poems of Wallace Stevens* (Vintage, 1990).

Part One Epigraph

T. S. Eliot, "Burnt Norton," in *T. S. Eliot: Collected Poems 1909–1962* (Harcourt, Brace & World, 1930).

Chapter Five

Margery Williams, *The Velveteen Rabbit* (Avon Books, 1975).

Part Two Epigraph

J. Krishnamurti, *Think on These Things* (HarperOne, 1989).

Part Three Epigraph

John O'Donohue, *Anam Cara: A Book of Celtic Wisdom* (Harper Collins, 1998).

Chapter Nineteen

Sogyal Rinpoche, *The Tibetan Book of Living and Dying* (HarperOne, 1994).

Chapter Twenty

T. S. Eliot, "Little Gidding," in *T. S. Eliot: Collected Poems 1909–1962* (Harcourt, Brace & World, 1930).

Epilogue

William Wordsworth, "Ode: Intimations of Immortality from Recollections of Early Childhood," in *William Wordsworth: Selected Poems and Prefaces* (Houghton Mifflin, 1965).

Afterword

Jan Frazier, *When Fear Falls Away: The Story of a Sudden Awakening* (Weiser Books, 2007).

Franklin Merrell-Wolff, *Pathways Through to Space* (Julian Press, 1973).

About the Author

At the age of fifty, Jan Frazier experienced a radical transformation of consciousness, bringing fear to an end and immersing her in a state of joyful well-being that has never left her. A widely published writer, she chronicled the unfolding changes in her awareness and in her experience of daily life. This account became *When Fear Falls Away: The Story of a Sudden Awakening* (Weiser Books, 2007). With the publication of that first book, Jan has become a teacher much sought after by others who long to leave behind the life of suffering. Her teachings are rooted in no particular tradition but come from her direct experience of the truth. In addition to her work as a spiritual teacher, Jan has continued to lead creative writing workshops in southern Vermont, where she lives. Her poetry and prose have appeared widely in literary journals and anthologies, and she has been nominated for a Pushcart Prize. She lives in southern Vermont. She is the mother of two young adults. Visit her at

www.JanFrazierTeachings.com.

To Our Readers

Weiser Books, an imprint of Red Wheel/Weiser, LLC, publishes books across the entire spectrum of occult, esoteric, speculative, and New Age subjects. Our mission is to publish quality books that will make a difference in people's lives without advocating any one particular path or field of study. We value the integrity, originality, and depth of knowledge of our authors.

Our readers are our most important resource, and we appreciate your input, suggestions, and ideas about what you would like to see published.

Visit our website at *www.redwheelweiser.com* to learn about our upcoming books and free downloads, and be sure to go to *www.redwheelweiser.com/newsletter/* to sign up for newsletters and exclusive offers.

You can also contact us at info@redwheelweiser.com or at

Red Wheel/Weiser
665 Third Street, Suite 400
San Francisco, CA 94107